EASY PREY

HOW TO PROTECT YOUR BUSINESS FROM DATA BREACH, CYBERCRIME AND EMPLOYEE FRAUD

Published by TechnologyPress, Orlando, FL.

TechnologyPress is a registered trademark.

Printed in the United States of America.

ISBN: 978-0-9966887-8-9
LCCN: 2016939556

This publication is designed to provide accurate and authoritative information with regard to the subject matter covered. It is sold with the understanding that the publisher is not engaged in rendering legal, accounting, or other professional advice. If legal advice or other expert assistance is required, the services of a competent professional should be sought. The opinions expressed by the authors in this book are not endorsed by TechnologyPress and are the sole responsibility of the author rendering the opinion.

Most TechnologyPress titles are available at special quantity discounts for bulk purchases for sales promotions, premiums, fundraising, and educational use. Special versions or book excerpts can also be created to fit specific needs.

For more information, please write:
TechnologyPress
520 N. Orlando Ave, #2
Winter Park, FL 32789
or call 1.877.261.4930

EASY PREY

HOW TO PROTECT YOUR BUSINESS FROM DATA BREACH, CYBERCRIME AND EMPLOYEE FRAUD

TechnologyPress
Winter Park, Florida

CONTENTS

PREFACE

By Robin Robins

YOU ARE A "SITTING DUCK"

You, the CEO of a small business, are under attack. Right now, extremely dangerous and well-funded cybercrime rings in China, Russia and the Ukraine are using sophisticated software systems to hack into thousands of small businesses like yours to steal credit cards, client information, and swindle money directly out of your bank account. Some are even being *funded by their own governments to attack American businesses.*

Don't think you're in danger because you're "small" and not a big target like a J.P. Morgan or Home Depot? Think again. 82,000 NEW malware threats are being released *every single day* and HALF of the cyber-attacks occurring are aimed at small businesses; you just don't hear about it because it's kept quiet for fear of attracting bad PR, lawsuits, data-breach fines and out of sheer *embarrassment.*

In fact, the National Cyber Security Alliance reports that one in five small businesses have been victims of cybercrime in the last year – and that number is *growing rapidly* as more businesses utilized cloud computing, mobile devices and store more information online. Quite simply, most small businesses are low-hanging fruit to hackers due to their lack of adequate security systems – **which is why I'm writing you today.**

I do realize that the above statements may come across as "fearmongering" and may upset you. That is *not* my intent. In fact, I personally know that the authors of this book are determined to WARN as many businesses as possible of the VERY REAL THREATS facing their organization so they have a chance to protect themselves and everything they've worked so hard to achieve.

When it comes to protecting your company, you need to know for certain – **without any lingering doubts** – that you are doing everything you can to avoid being an easy target for cybercriminals. In my admittedly informal survey, talking to hundreds of CEOs who have been hacked or compromised, almost all of them told me they thought their IT guy "had things covered."

As a business owner myself, I understand that you can't do *everything*. You have to delegate and trust, at some level, that your employees and vendors are doing the right thing – **but it never hurts to get the facts yourself and validate that they are.**

You've spent a lifetime working hard to get where you are. No one gave you anything. You earned every penny and every client through honest means – not to mention a stellar reputation. Don't let some low-life thief operating outside the law get away with taking that from you. Get the facts from this book and *be certain* that you are protected.

Robin Robins, CEO, Technology Marketing Toolkit, Inc.

CHAPTER 1

SMALL BUSINESSES
A CYBERCRIMINAL'S EASIEST PREY

BY DARREN COLEMAN

There are two kinds of companies: those that have been hacked and those that will be.
~ Former FBI Director, Robert S. Mueller III

CYBERCRIME

It's a word that most of us have heard of but many *believe* we're exempt from. *Nothing could be further from the truth!* Everyone has the potential to be the victim of a cyber attack, and no one is more vulnerable than small businesses; especially real estate brokerages, law offices, and accounting firms.

Are you wondering why small businesses are such a lucrative target for these virtual criminals? The answer is quite simple—*many small business owners do not believe that the information they have is of any real value to anyone but themselves.* It's this false perception that has created a relentless and growing criminal industry. Cybercriminals never stop, not even when they are sleeping, because their computers are continuously working for them. They are eager to invade any business that they find vulnerable due to a lack of practical layers of defense in their technology.

In order to better understand "why" a small business's information is of so much value to these perpetrators, you need to first understand what cybercrime is. *Cybercrime is defined as any criminal activity that involves the Internet, a computer system, or computer technology.* A pretty basic definition, for certain. It encompasses a great many things. Here are just a few of the ways that cybercrime can impact your business on a daily basis:

- Identity theft—stealing employee or client information.
- Phishing—finding ways to voluntarily be given information or to get it via compromised email links.
- Spamming—in order to sell illegal or fraudulent products that "get them" the money.
- Theft of your intellectual property—cybercriminals are smart, but they are often lazy, preferring to take what someone's already created.
- Stealing information and funds from online bank and financial accounts—if they find a way to get to your funds, they will, and you will likely never see those monies again.
- Distributing malware to a targeted system or many different systems—malware can ruin technology systems or shut down businesses completely for detrimental periods of time.
- Finding confidential information and posting it to the Internet— some cybercrime is about creating minor and major disruptions (WikiLeaks, for example).
- Holding critical information on your computer(s) for ransom—you pay or never see it again.
- Attacking network infrastructures—crippling a business through its unprotected technology.

The above list is only the tip of the iceberg! There are no holidays from cybercrime. Each and every day is an opportunity for a cybercriminal to get a bit more inventive about what they can find virtually to exploit for their own gain.

WHY SMALL BUSINESSES ARE A CYBERCRIMINAL'S "EASY PICKINGS"

It is estimated that 40% of a small business' net worth is derived from the information it owns.

There is an incredible amount of risk that is not being addressed by small business owners. It's astounding that 77% of businesses do not even have an Internet Security Policy in place for employees, which means that they are really "hoping" that their employees will not open a bad link or wire funds to a party that isn't a legitimate business partner. Approximately 63% of small businesses have no policies in place on Social Media use within their workplace—this is certainly an effective way to invite cybercrime in. Those numbers are staggering to me.

Data is such a valuable commodity these days and with 45% of businesses not even offering Internet safety training for their employees, these businesses are ideal candidates for the cybercriminals. Furthermore, there is an even greater chance that the business may not even be aware that a cybercriminal has invaded their network for quite some time.

Small business owners often do not set aside the necessary funds within their budget for proper technology defenses, often viewing them as both "costly and unnecessary defenses," feeling those monies are better spent elsewhere. Or perhaps they are lacking in:

- Time
- Expertise to implement security defenses
- An IT specialist on the payroll
- Risk awareness
- Employee training
- Updated systems to prevent cyber attacks
- Secure endpoints

When the defenses are down, the vulnerability can be easily exposed. Due to automation, cybercriminals can mass produce attacks with very little investment.

There are staggering stories out there about businesses that experienced significant loss (personally and financially) or were even completely shut down after a cyber breach. In some cases, they could not come back from the disaster, either due to lack of trust from their clients or because the loss was that significant.

Here's a real life example of what a cybercriminal did to one company: There was a California escrow company with nine employees whose system became compromised without their knowledge. Escrow accounts have a significant amount of money that is streamed through them for real estate transactions. Three requests were made from this escrow company to their bank to wire $500,000.00 overseas, one in December 2012, and two in January 2013. The bank had a system in place where they provided two factor authentication; however, the system was down at that time. They chose to send those wires, anyway, despite this escrow company never having transferred funds overseas. *The result of this hack and rapid loss of $1.5 million dollars was that the escrow company was placed in receivership*—a type of corporate bankruptcy where a receiver is appointed by the bankruptcy courts or creditors to run the company. Ultimately, these receivers usually are given the decision-making powers over all the assets and their management. This escrow company did not have the proper cyber training in place or good security defenses. A costly error that created a damaged reputation and nine employees being out of a job.

Examples like the escrow company's dilemma above are more prevalent than what many may think. In fact, according to a 2013 Ernst and Young survey, 96% of small businesses are unprepared for a cyber attack. For businesses such as escrow accounts and real estate brokerages, this is a particularly big deal—they have highly detailed information on thousands of individuals. *This type of scare is meant to alarm small businesses with the singular purpose of motivating them to acknowledge that their assets are valuable to cybercriminals.* We all can relate to protecting what we place value on, whether it's a possession, our loved ones, or in this case—our livelihood.

CREATE A CYBER SECURITY SOLUTION

There are smart and effective moves that will help small businesses protect their interests that can be done—starting today!

Common sense solutions that factor in all areas with regards to a threat to technology does exist. Will some of them require an investment? Yes, they will; however, compared with a small business being attacked and either having to close its doors or "start all over," an investment in the right defenses is not only smart; it's also much more affordable than you think. Here's how you can get started:

1. **Employee awareness:** employees use the technology that make a small business run, which means that a great many things are in their control. As an expert on helping small businesses (like those real estate brokerages) protect themselves, I offer my clients' employees training on the fundamentals of cyber security, including:

   - Why having network monitoring and alerts is important
   - The reasons that your computer should automatically lock after a few short minutes of not being in use
   - Explanations as to what can go awry when sensitive information is transmitted via email
   - Why it is imperative to use a VPN (Virtual Private Network) when you are using a public Wi-Fi system
   - How to create and implement an Internet Security Plan in case a cyber security crisis happens
   - Safe data practices
   - How to recognize malicious links that may contain malware
   - Understanding the specifics of safe passwords per Passwords Policy for business, which will include:
     - 10 characters or longer password
     - No dictionary works
     - Complex rules that utilize upper case, lower case, numbers, and symbols (!@#$%, etc.)
     - A passphrase (ex: @uapiasifab! = using a passphrase is a smart idea for any business)
     - Two factor authentication (when available)
     - Checking password for strength (sites such as passfault.com)
   - Email security that will:
     - Teach employees to never click on a link in an email (it's always safer to type the address manually)
     - Create mindfulness about not opening up email attachments from unknown or unconfirmed sources
     - Help employees to identify phishing emails that usually look realistic, or have attached .zip files that will spread a virus through a single computer or an entire system rapidly
   - Aside from using a dedicated computer for banking transactions,

do your research to see what online banking safeguards various institutions have in place. Their policies do impact you! Look for:

- ◆ Two factor authentication
- ◆ Treasury management
- ◆ Bank alert and notification policies
- ◆ Who is responsible for unauthorized transactions
- ◆ Knowing what banking Trojans exist to get your information

The best technology in the world is far less effective if employees are not properly trained on how it will protect the business' assets and what they need to do with it, specifically.

2. **Physical security:** not everything that is associated with cybercrime prevention comes through a virtual connection or an employee's decisions. There are practical steps that can be taken with the physical space in which equipment is housed, helping to protect it from those criminals who are bold enough to actually pay your business a visit. It is highly recommended to:

- Keep the server(s) in a locked room or closet
- Pay attention to any guests or visitors who will be unescorted (particularly ones who you do not have an established working relationship with)
- Put in place policies against mobile workers leaving their laptops in plain sight in their vehicles, or unattended in public places
- Have systems in place to verify if information is being loaded onto USB drives by employees (associated with intellectual property theft)
- Use data encryption to secure all information against loss or theft in event that a computer is stolen or infected

There have been instances where hackers would dress up like an IT person or some other professional, walk right into a business with the assumption that they wouldn't be properly vetted. They would quite literally go and place a virus on a business's server or download data from it. This is easily avoided once you are aware of the potential risks.

3. IT professional functions: IT professionals like me are passionate about knowing everything going on with technology and staying up to date on the latest risks, trends, and concerns. We have instant access to valuable data like this, whereas many businesses do not. Evaluating how everything is going "once in a while" or "when you have time" is not effective for prevention. What if something goes wrong the day after your last check and you don't discover it for a month? This is where Coleman Technologies really shines for our clients, by offering:

- Security software installation on all computers, keeping it both updated with the latest patches and at maximum function
- Installing hardware firewalls to block outside attacks
- Installing intrusion detection systems, which will detect attacks from both outside the organization and inside the network
- Helping to create Password and Internet User Policies, Disaster Recovery Plans, and educating employees on why they are important, while providing a blueprint to restore information as quickly as possible, should a breach occur
- Setting up email encryption to help ensure that data transmitted via email is safe and secure from hackers
- Continual monitoring of logs and virtual paper trails to look for suspect activity
- Making sure that the web browsers being used are the most up-to-date versions available—these updates often include patches (or fixes) to problems that hackers discovered in the browser itself

Part of what makes Coleman Technologies highly efficient and effective at what we do is that we get to know the businesses and employees that we work with very well, assessing how they conduct business and what their risks may be. Then we come up with practical strategies and applications that will help them have the type of security in place that cybercriminals will likely avoid. They'll move on to the easier targets. While there is no 100% solution, there are many ways to minimize the impact of a breach.

WE'VE BEEN BREACHED! WHAT NEXT?
Your actions and expediency are critical if you've been hacked.

A business that is paralyzed because they've been hacked is a business at risk. Their chances of surviving the event rely on how organized they are "in case of emergency" and the swiftness of their response. There are four things that must be addressed.

1. Take affected computers offline immediately. If you are not sure which ones are affected, take them all offline until someone who can make that determination is present.
2. Call an IT professional and have them come in and begin to assess the situation.
3. Review the drive before any attempts to restore or reboot the system are done, and if at all possible, purchase a new drive rather than restoring the existing, affected one.
4. Report the incident to the police. Even if they cannot solve the crime, the information that they can collect from breaches due to cybercrime is valuable in helping establish trends, patterns, vulnerabilities, and information. Plus, insurance companies usually require a police file number.

A breach will never be a welcomed occurrence, but you cannot ask for any more "ideal" method of recovery than the four steps listed above. Using IT professionals will help reduce the stress and improve the recovery time—especially when the right plans, policies, and training are in place.

SAY GOODBYE TO THE DAYS OF BEING EASY PREY

If you think of your small business's ability to avoid a cyber attack without the proper measures in place as a Las Vegas bet, you'd find that no one is going to think the odds are in your favor. Look, I get how it can be overwhelming, but with the right IT partnership in place, it becomes a bit easier. I encourage you to visit: www.ColemanTechnologies.com/cybersecurity to learn as much as you can about this "hard to keep up with" illegal activity known as cybercrime.

You've worked hard to build your business. That's why protecting your data assets from a breach is imperative. I get this, and it drives the way Coleman Technologies operates. **This is why we will always work hard for you!**

About Darren

Darren Coleman is a passionate Information Technology Professional, Entrepreneur, and Technology Author based in Langley, British Columbia, Canada. Currently, he is the President and Certified IT Administrator for Coleman Technologies, which he founded in 1999.

Throughout the span of nearly two decades, Darren has acquired extensive expertise in the world of Information Technology and has directly worked with some of the top real estate franchises in the nation. As a Technical Specialist in a multitude of areas, his key fortes lie in Consulting, IT Management Services, Computer Security, and more.

Darren's avid interest in technology has led to his extensive training and many certifications in areas such as Information Technology and Computer Support Specialist (ITCSS), Certified Ethical Hacker (CEH), and Datto Certified Advance Technician. He also possesses his CompTIA A+ and CompTIA Network + qualifications and has completed extensive training in Linux Administration & Configuration.

When he isn't immersed in his career, Darren enjoys travelling and spending time outdoors with family and friends. Most importantly, Darren enjoys nothing more than spending quality time with his lovely wife and children. He and his wife are the proud parents of three beautiful girls.

CHAPTER 2

HISTORY OF CYBERCRIME

BY MICHAEL BUBERNACK

In today's technology-driven world, cybercrime is a word repeated frequently throughout the justice system. A cybercrime is any crime that occurs within the digital world. These may include, but are not limited to, the creation of malware or viruses, phishing, hacking, ransomware, buying or selling any illegal goods, whether it be credit card information or illicit substances, and installing malware or viruses. Cybercrime has been constantly evolving and improving, especially following the creation of the Internet. Though the USA Patriot Act of 2001 reduced these crimes greatly, cybercrime is one of the greatest grossing crimes today. From the time of creation of the computer up to the invention of smartphones, cybercrime has been a pervasive issue.

1970 – 1975

The year is 1971, present day technologies such as the Internet or even instant messaging would be considered as something straight out of a science fiction movie. For many Americans in this time period, computers are brand new, complex technologies, taking up entire rooms, only to be considered largely by the elite. This, however, didn't prevent crime from being committed using them.

John Draper was enjoying his breakfast cereal in his Las Vegas home when he found a toy whistle in his box of Captain Crunch. This whistle would put Draper down in history as one of the first recorded cybercriminals. His spark of genius occurred when he discovered this whistle created sounds at a perfect 2600 Hertz tone. Draper soon got to work creating his blue box, which would enable him to create a sound along with his blue box that could be projected into a public phone receiver and allow the user to make phone calls for free. A popular men's magazine, Esquire, picked up Draper story, complete with instructions for readers to create their own "blue boxes," causing phone fraud to skyrocket around the U.S. While John Draper was creating his blue box, one of the very first rogue programs, titled "creeper," stormed throughout pioneering bulletin board networks, wreaking havoc on entire computer systems.

One year later, the very first bill was passed with the means of governing the standards of the Internet, then in its infancy and still far out of reach of the general population. It's creator, Vinton Cerf, is now hailed as the "Father of the Internet." Though this may have seemed minor and went generally unnoticed by the public during the year of its release, this bill would later be a large staple in the Internet's, as well as the country's history. Since its implementation, dozens of laws have been instituted to govern and secure the vast and complex modern Internet. Though many of these bills have remained controversial in the public's eye, if left completely unpoliced, the Internet may have been unusable by the public today.

With evolving technologies, theft on a large scale with the Internet as a medium was simply a ticking time bomb. In 1973, big banks largely ruled the American economy, with New York as epicenter, though the fact that a scandal was executed successfully by a simple bank teller remains a wonder. New York's Dime Savings Bank was at the time worth millions, and unlike many other companies, had already implemented the usage of computer systems in their businesses, a critical mistake on their part, as the bank teller mentioned was able to embezzle a staggering two million dollars through the cyber world. Though later caught and convicted, this crime was undoubtedly the first crime of its kind.

1975 – 1980

The first Personal Computer, the Altair 8800, has already been put on the market for mass and relatively cheap sale, and an increasing number of Americans have access to a computer in their daily lives. The year is 1978, and the first black market of the cyber world appeared as an electronic bulletin board system (BBS). This became the primary means of communications between criminals via computer. This could be compared to the dark web of today, though it was far smaller and lesser known at the time of its existence.

Three years into the future, "Captain Zappy," whose common name was Ian Murphy, becomes infamous in a large scale hacking scandal. Hacking was increasing in popularity, and like today, many of the offenders weren't searching for wealth but instead for recognition in making a statement and gaining popularity for achieving a reputation for hacking and causing digital destruction. Think of the modern day term of "Hackers Anonymous" and apply it to the year 1981. Murphy's crime was extremely simple, yet cost the company, AT&T, thousands of dollars in revenue. Ian Murphy simply changed the time on the electronic billing clock within their systems, allowing an enormous number of customers to receive the discounts they would only be granted outside of normal business hours around the clock. Captain Zappy was later traced and convicted of the very first felony charge pertaining to any cybercrime.

Almost every reader has contracted a virus on their computer, whether it was from opening an infected email or mistakenly browsing a dangerous website – yet only a few years ago, viruses were virtually unheard of. That is, until the creation of "Elk Cloner," a devastating virus released approximately sometime during 1982. It was considered to be an Apple boot virus, wherein the infected computer would malfunction upon being turned "on," though it cost consumers hundreds of thousands of dollars. IBM PCs (any computer system not manufactured by Macintosh) remained unscathed by the virus, perhaps contributing to Apple's now strictly secure operating systems.

Though hacking was indisputably present at the time, when the blockbuster hit "Wargames" was released in 1983, hacking was discovered by many average citizens in a way it had never been before – through the explanation of "war dialing." Since its release, dozens of movies have been made on the topics of both hacking and cybercrimes in a general sense, being an everyday part of the media as well as pop culture.

Another notable event that occurred in 1983 was the implementation of a law which granted the Secret Service the right to charge citizens in the event of either computer or credit card fraud. Today, fraud is one of the most common as well as top-grossing cybercrimes. Phishing programs may steal information by sending false emails claiming to be banks or unions; viruses and malware may be able to access login information stored on a person's computer, and false advertisements for claiming free prizes may ask for personal information as well. When obtaining information, many programmers will sell this information either on the black market or to a third party vendor, as well as using it for their own personal gain. It has become such a pressing issue, in fact, the majority of us will have either our identity or credit card information stolen within our adult lifetimes.

1984 was a relatively eventful year in cybercrime history, encompassing the Masters of Deception, the U.S. Comprehensive Control Act, and Hacker magazine. Scalable hacking teams were uncommon during the 1980's, and until the Masters of Deception, it was considered a solitary crime by many. Phiber Optik, however, changed the standards, creating his own infamous hacking team which was covered by many of America's main media outlets.

By '84, several acts were already instituted protecting the welfare of computer users in the U.S. In an attempt to validate the guidelines published the previous year granting the secret service full permission to prosecute cyber fraud, Washington passed the historical Comprehensive Control act.

Still in print today, the popular Hacker Magazine, 2600, is published and released to the population on a large scale, welcoming regular people with little prior knowledge to attempt to hack themselves, and again making hacking more commonplace and far beyond a small group of highly knowledgeable criminals as it were previously.

1985 – 1990

Following the hit magazine of the previous year, a more in-depth, selective, and far less popular magazine was published digitally in 1985, titled, Phrack.

To this day, IBM computers are primarily produced not for personal leisurely use, but as systems for businesses to take advantage of, creating far more efficient cash registers and check out systems, medical appointment and file systems, just to name a few of the products offered.

Though their popularity decreased in the 2010's, many companies still take advantage of their niche technologies. In their heyday in 1986, they were the target of a largely destructive virus named "Pakistani Brain," the first of its kind to not be created legally in the eyes of the government, giving the attack it's notoriety in history.

The Computer Emergency Response Team was enacted during 1987, consisting of educated professionals who had the knowledge and the means to continually improve the security as well as the resilience for America's computers as a whole. It was funded and was created by the Software Engineering Institute, both of which are still in service.

As years passed and computers have become a greater and greater part of American lifestyles, the number of notable crimes increased, as well as is covered increasingly in the media. An example of one such crime occurred in 1988, though it was a relatively petty crime and carried an extremely short sentence for Kevin Mitnick, the offender. The monitoring of both DEC and MCI personal emails was closely followed by media outlets, and as a result Mitnick became a quite infamous criminal.

Ironically, the second great cybercrime during '88 was also committed by another Kevin, Kevin Poulsen, who is recognized more for his escape and avoidance of the law than his actual crime. Phone tampering is a relatively common crime, just as it was several decades ago, but when Poulsen was eventually tracked down and a warrant was issued for his arrest, he was able to go into hiding for a staggering seventeen months before he was eventually found and convicted in a court of law.

We've already visited the 1973 embezzlement of a couple million dollars, which shocked a New York bank, yet the following crime makes the '73 embezzlement seem almost insignificant. For this time around, in 1988, there were a couple more dollars at stake—how much exactly? Try seventy million dollars, robbed from the First National Bank of Chicago, again completely digitally.

As the son of the prestigious Chief Scientist at NSA, Robert T. Morris was a highly educated individual, receiving a graduate degree from Cornell University. Unfortunately for him, intelligence doesn't always go hand in hand with morality and compassion. Morris found himself sentenced with three years' probation along with a hefty fine of ten thousand dollars. In addition to this, Morris was expelled from his school and was relatively unsuccessful for the remainder of his life. Though his crimes were horrendous, Morris was undeniably a genius in his own right.

By this time, a precursor to the Internet has been invented, though it gained little traction in the long run, and was titled ARPA net. Morris invented a highly successful self-replicating worm which he then releases on this Internet outline, infecting and junking over 6,000 computer systems, many of those owned by wealthy universities and governmental institutions. Though it had not been his intention to create such a devastating program, Morris was identified and recognized by the media at the time for the vastness of his worm.

During the late 1980's, the AIDS epidemic was at an all-time high, causing social tension between homosexual victims and the rest of society as the threat of death was almost certain when the virus was contracted, and with no research to conclude exactly how the virus was spread, many simply blamed the homosexual population for its spread. So when an "AIDS quiz" was published during 1989, many unsuspecting victims downloaded the program without a second thought, and that is how the very first cyber extortion case was created. Upon download, a virus would attack the computer system, demanding $500 be paid to a foreign account if the user wished to retain access—similar to the ransomware that is increasingly encountered today.

1991 – PRESENT DAY

The landscape of cybercrime changes daily. There are still hackers, viruses, and malware to contend with, but there are newer forms of cybercrime. Ransomware is a virus that affects your computer and demands that you pay a ransom (often in untraceable bitcoins) in order to access your encrypted data. Smart Phones and smart credit cards are the newest targets in which cybercriminals can steal information by just being in proximity of you.

As technology advances, the way to leverage cybercrime advances as well, and for organized crime syndicates, terrorists and even teenagers looking for a thrill, the digital world is ripe with opportunity.

About Michael

Michael Bubernack has been working in the original family business all his life. Now a proud co-owner (with his wife Fusun), and CEO of ET&T, Inc. from Lehigh Valley, Pennsylvania, the company was formed 48 years ago to provide an alternative for companies to acquire business telephone systems. The Interconnect Industry, as it was known, provided competition to the Bell Systems. ET&T was formed just after the FCC's Carter-phone Decision (1968) which proclaimed private telephone devices could be hooked up to the public telephone network. Businesses no longer had to rent from the monopoly. ET&T continues to provide "Service You Trust" since 1968.

Mike always enjoyed working with technology and earned a Bachelor's degree in Computer Science and Business Administration. Learning machine language and coding on DEC mainframe computers was not what Mike envisioned, but Business Administration and providing solutions to business was more important, and where things really clicked.

The first computer for the business was acquired in 1981. It was nothing like what is provided today. The same goes for the big, heavy and expensive phone systems. Mike's experience, spanning almost five decades, has resulted in business transformation to the cloud, with computers and telephone systems along with managed services and support. Top of mind is business continuity and secure computing.

In the late 80's, ET&T competed and won a State contract from 'Ma Bell' for services on the embedded base of old phone systems. Today, ET&T continues to hold State Contracts for premise-based phone systems and Master IT Contract Services for networking. Over the years, Mike and the ET&T Team have installed and or fixed thousands of networks. Their focus naturally is geared toward service and maintenance of their customer's technology including telephone and computing systems. For new projects, the company is an independent consulting distributor of technology for business, government and institutional organizations. ET&T, with their team of highly dedicated and trained employees, boasts of their local, long-time customers.

From copper cables for mechanical systems, electronic and then digital phones systems, and 300 Baud to faster-than-lightning Internet connections using fiber optics, highlights Mike's experience for computing and VOIP. Mike and the company have seen it all the way to the ubiquitous wireless technologies available today. His main belief has always been to keep the network up and running for their customers. It is the reason they've been able to stay in business, and will be the basis for their continued success. Customer service is not everything, it is the only thing for their clients.

In addition to working in the secure technology field, Mike enjoys the outdoors and woodworking as a hobby. Mike and Fusun have been able to raise two successful daughters, and hope that one day they will have in interest in taking ET&T to even greater success for the third generation of the family business.

Mike can be contacted at:
- 610-433-1000,
- mbubernack@et-t.com
- www.ET-T.com

CHAPTER 3

WHO ARE THE BAD GUYS?
– THE MEANS AND MOTIVES OF CYBERCRIME

By JOHN RUTKOWSKI, BOLDER Designs

It's talked about and publicized, but people are still resistant to "getting it." The it that I am speaking of is cybersecurity and how it is necessary to protect resources, both for business and individuals. *For some reason, despite an alarming rate of stories about cybercrime and its dire consequences, many business owners in particular still say, "Well, that won't happen to me."* It's a dangerous ideology to subscribe to, because your chances of getting blindsided are high.

To put it into perspective, just imagine… You come home from work one day and there's a squatter in your house. They've made themselves at home and are cooking a nice meal, using your resources. They've used your food, tools, and electricity. They plan on eating that meal on your couch and not even sharing any of it with you. **To them—it's theirs, not yours.** This is what the bad guys are doing with technology—sneaking in through a back door and taking over, claiming what you have for their own purposes. They are network squatters and they are exceptionally smart and dedicated to their career path of crime.

UNDERSTANDING THE "BAD GUYS"
"I rob banks because that's where the money is."
~ Willy Sutton, Famous Criminal

The bad guys know exactly where to go for the information they need. **For bank robbers like Willy Sutton, you go to the bank, but for cybercriminals, they go to the technology that businesses use to get what's of value to them.** This information has value and they will sell it to other criminals, who will create enormous chaos in the lives of the victims. The theft of data and resources leads to:

1. **Identity theft:** someone becomes you and soaks your good credit dry as quickly as they can, even purchasing homes under your name. If you're lucky, it's just a single transaction that you have to recover from!

2. **Financial data theft:** accessing financial data to divert funds to the criminals.

3. **Password theft:** email passwords are valuable to the bad guys. Gaining access to them allows someone to send spam emails with malicious links to their contact list, while also encouraging people to share confidential data such as phone numbers, Social Media log-ins, etc. For professionals, the seriousness of this is escalated because they could suffer damage to their reputation.

There are some staggering statistics on what groups of individuals actually make up the category we lump together as "bad guys" for cybercrime. It's easy to see that any of these organizations could do great harm with the right information in their hands.

- 70 percent individuals or small groups
- 20 percent criminal organizations
- 5 percent cyber terrorists
- 4 percent state-sponsored players
- 1 percent hacktivists ("pseudo cyber armies," not Anonymous)

State sponsored cybercrime: Countries use cybercrime to suppress dissention, promote their agenda, and to defend interests.

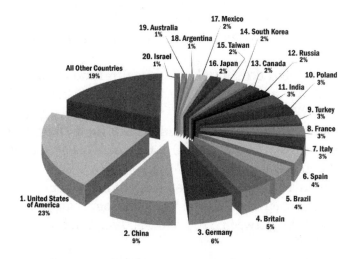

Cybercrime: Top 20 Countries

Figure 1.

Organized crime: many people think of drugs, alcohol, and other shady endeavors as being a part of organized crimebut cybercrime is a very profitable market for them—and one that is hard to trace if done correctly.

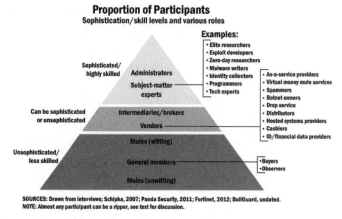

Figure 2.

Reselling data: the black Internet is a place where criminals can do commerce—buying and purchasing stolen data and even high tech kits that will allow them to enter into the cybercrime business.

♦ **Average estimated price for stolen credit and debit cards:** $5 to $30 in the US; $20 to $35 in the UK; $20 to $40 in Canada;

$21 to $40 in Australia; and $25 to $45 in the European Union

* **Bank login credentials for a $2,200 balance bank account:** $190

* **Bank login credentials plus stealth funds transfers to US banks:** from $500 for a $6,000 account balance, to $1,200 for a $20,000 account balance

* **Bank login credentials and stealth funds transfers to UK banks:** from $700 for a $10,000 account balance, to $900 for a $16,000 account balance

* **Login credentials for online payment services such as PayPal:** between $20 and $50 for account balances from $400 to $1,000; between $200 and $300 for balances from $5,000 to $8,000

* **Login credentials to hotel loyalty programs and online auction accounts:** $20 to $1,400

* **Login credentials for online premium content services such as Netflix:** as little as $0.55

Bad guys are committed to creating problems for businesses or individuals and don't stop their pursuits easily. Think of the classic movie Butch Cassidy and the Sundance Kid. There's a scene in there that expresses the mindset of cybercriminals masterfully:

Butch Cassidy: *How many are following us?*
Sundance Kid: *All of 'em.*
Butch Cassidy: *All of 'em? What's the matter with those guys?*

It's easy to think that these types of criminals must have something better to do with their time, but this type of pursuit is the best use of their time, because they are going to experience a certain level of success.

Tip for Protecting Resources: The bad guys try to drive you crazy—realize this! They will send you "urgent" correspondence that requires immediate action, hoping that you'll be so busy that you don't question it at all. They want you to click on those bad links because once you do, they are in control. For example, if you get a notification that you need to take immediate action for a shipment from Australia via FedEx, you'd want to consider if you have even ordered anything from Australia for starters. And in addition, ask:

- **Why are they sending it?** With your position, evaluate if you have a solid reason to receive that type of email.
- **Was I expecting it?** Emails that fall from your standard daily operations should automatically be suspect.
- **Do I know its purpose?** When a request is "out-of-the-ordinary," don't hesitate to ask the proper people—usually in a position that is higher up than yours—if they know about it, and in many cases, it may be verifying that they indeed sent the email.

TECHNOLOGY DOESN'T LIE

Never assume trust with an email, even one that appears to come from someone else within your organization—particularly if the request is not "business as usual."

Technology does what it's told to do; it doesn't act of its own accord. It's when we add in the human factor—whether it is an actual error from a good person or a deliberate act of sabotage from a bad guy—that we run into troubles! Although he was part of an entirely different era, it seems that Butch really did understand the mentality of today's bad guys best. After wondering, what's the matter with those guys, he told us this:

I couldn't do that. Could you do that? Why can they do it? Who are those guys?

What makes someone so determined to continue their pursuit of someone or something? It requires skills that we often associate with good results, such as focus, dedication, and confidence that they'll succeed. **And many times, the bad guys do succeed!** Why? Because they are hard to track. Even if a lone hacker (called a Script Kiddie) gets an intrusion and collects data, they are not going to personally use it. They are going to sell it quickly—and then move on. It's hard to track down who they are, even. Many times, it's impossible. So there's some big confidence going on here, right? And their career in crime is lucrative, as well, because these bad guys run good looking businesses, including bonuses, recruitment campaigns, and even holiday parties! It's very empowering and the longer you can remain active in cybercrime, the bolder you get.

SOCIAL ENGINEERING IS WHAT MAKES IT ALL POSSIBLE

Social engineering preys on a business's employees because they are the greatest security problem within the organization.

Social engineering is the art of manipulating people to give up confidential information. It is highly dangerous because the people that are giving up that information have no idea what is happening to them at that moment. They find out when it's too late—the problem has already exploded into something big.

Think of a tree when you think of social engineering. It all starts with one compromised individual (the trunk). Someone breaks into their technology and gains access to something and in an instant, sends out say 4,000 emails with malicious links, to people. Even if 1% of those people open that up, that is 40 people who become the initial person's branches and a trunk themselves. *Now the bad guy is sending out emails like mad—all in the blink of an eye—because technology is working for him.* It goes on and on, until suddenly, that branched out tree is really like a forest full of cybercrime. It's hard to stop and equally challenging to keep up with. **Unless…you train humans to know what to look for!**

As humans, we tend to make assumptions based on what we believe is going on, often not paying a lot of attention to possible threats. This is extra true when we are in a comfortable environment. Let me share the story of the valet with you. This couple, who ate at the same restaurant once a week, every week for the past ten years, pulled up one night. They were excited about the new service when someone came up and asked, **"Can I have the keys to your car to go park it?"** *They smiled, liking the extra touch the restaurant now offered, and handed the keys over.* Once inside the restaurant, they had their usual casual conversation with the manager and mentioned how they really appreciated the valet service the restaurant now offered. The manager was a bit surprised and said, "I'm not certain what you're talking about." The couple explained and the manager had to tell them that whoever the valet was, he was not affiliated with their restaurant. **In essence, this customer just handed over his keys to a criminal—unknowingly but without question.**

This is exactly what happens when people offer information via the Internet, assuming that it's a certain person or party. The "so-called valet" probably got $5,000.00 for handing over a $100,000 Mercedes, and everyone else that touched it after that got a bit of money, too. Everyone won, except the guy whose car got stolen. **When a business gets compromised and resources or data are stolen, the only people that win are the bad guys.** Don't let the bad guys win!

Spear-phishing is a form of social engineering where specific people are targeted within an organization in hopes that they will hand over something of value. Most often, they seek money through this route. The scenario goes something like this:

> Company ACME is a great company, showing all the employees on their website and giving a bit of information about them. It's their marketing plan and they want to be accessible to potential customers. The CEO of the company is a "get it done quick" individual, making decisions quickly and not afraid to go bold. That's his nature. The accountant is someone he relies on to ensure that funds get to where they need to be quickly.

> One day, the accountant receives an email from the CEO that $9,873.27 needs to be wired to a party that's overseas and it needs to be done as quickly as possible to secure a deposit for a new deal. It's unique, in that it's the first international deal ever for this company. But not wanting to ruffle feathers or be responsible for a lost opportunity the accountant does as requested. Later that day, they bring it up to the CEO. Guess what? The CEO is clueless, and that $9,873.27 is already gone, and unlikely to be traceable or returned at any point.

Scenarios like that listed above are happening every day to businesses, impacting them significantly. Real estate firms and escrow companies are particularly vulnerable, as they deal in high dollar amounts. If you don't have insurance in place to help you recover from a loss due to this type of theft, it could ruin the business you work for. A ruined business turns into a closed business, which means that the only certainty you'll have is job hunting. So remember, voluntarily giving anyone anything, whether it's legitimate or not, often means that you will not be able to recover those lost funds via insurance of any sort.

All businesses that rely on technology in any capacity should seek out a cyber insurance company to start a conversation with about cyber insurance. During this conversation you will want to:

- Find out how coverage works for things outside of the realm of "voluntary theft"
- Ask what the policies are if fraud is involved in any way
- Learn what the limits and deductibles are for the various options
- Get the details of what—exactly—you'll be covered for in case of cyber theft

BOLDER MOVES LEAD TO BIGGER PREVENTION
Reducing the risk cybercrime due to human error and lack of knowledge is something that BOLDER Design advocates for consistently.

If I could reach out to every business owner or decision maker and have a heart-to-heart about how important it is to understand who the bad guys are, I'd do it in an instant. For now, as a 'service to my clients' and to those who follow me on my various Social Media sites, I create awareness through blogs and articles that are posted regularly to my Facebook and LinkedIn Pages (see bio for website details).

Creating awareness of what these bad guys are hoping to achieve— exactly—is a way that I can help everyone, not just my clients, practice smarter, safer business. *When businesses succeed and keep the bad guys at bay, the good guys win.* **That sounds pretty great to me!**

About John

John Rutkowski has successfully launched, operated and managed four businesses so far in his business career. While the types of businesses might seem unrelated, they have all dealt with building solutions for a client's problems.

He has the knack for seeing the flaw in a pile of perfection. But then again, it's not perfect. His education started with a lot of family travel, while he never moved from the family home, he had visited most of the lower 48 states before high school. He believes in the motto: Travel exposes you to new ideas, culture and thinking.

At the University of Virginia he studied Architecture, following in the family business, but ended up with a B.S. in Commerce. "I was the long-haired hippy in the business school." But that lead him to be the first in his class to have a job offer before graduation. John founded BOLDER Designs in 1986 with the then new solution of CAD software for Architects and Engineers. Being that such clients need to collaborate he built up his business around the networking of such clients and provided solutions to their growing Branch Office and Remote Worker needs. Hence this chapter in the book.

It is said that you become the people you hang out with, John is proud to be a contributor along with the other authors of this book. He has grown through their contributions to the book and looks forward to writing another one with them.

John has spoken nationally at numerous technology events, giving keynotes on how to transform and grow your business.

You can connect with John at:
- me@JohnRutkowski.com
- www.linkedin.com/in/johnrutkowski
- https://www.facebook.com/BolderDesigns

And the business LinkedIn page:
- https://www.linkedin.com/company/bolder-designs).

CHAPTER 4

THE TOP TEN SECURITY CONCERNS FOR SMALL BUSINESSES

BY LARRY BURBANO

Many of us are falsely under the assumption that cybercriminals primarily target larger corporations, due to the fact that large firms may offer greater rewards when breached. Although this is fairly true, it is actually small businesses that harbor the greatest security concerns, especially for businesses with two hundred or fewer employees. There are several factors contributing to this. Foremost, many small businesses lack both the finances and materials to properly secure themselves, as opposed to larger businesses with larger budgets.

Many larger businesses have implemented an Acceptable Usage Policy (AUP), which is essentially a legally binding document all employees must follow pertaining to all their device usage connected to their employers. This is not something small businesses would implement because they would not feel it is necessary. Sometimes small businesses are small, tight-knit groups that feel like family, and so the idea that anyone would do anything that could jeopardize the company, whether intentional or not, is a foreign concept to them.

In addition, many corporations hire outside agencies to deal with all of their security concerns, ensuring they are protected by professionally knowledgeable persons. Top of the line antivirus and anti-malware programs may be extremely costly, especially because in most cases several security programs are necessary to provide the right level of cyber security coverage.

Terminating old employee accounts, emails, and any electronic ties to a company is also less commonplace in small businesses, putting them at greater risk. Cyber Security protocols may seem extremely intimidating to many small businesses, and the fact that knowledge of what to do to protect a small business is not common. In this chapter following, you will learn about the top security concerns, as well as relatively simple solutions that are applicable in real life.

EVERY DAY ACTIONS

The foremost security concern for small businesses is the everyday actions of employees. The majority of breaches that occur in small businesses happen due to the access of an unsafe website, email, or download. When security isn't at the forefront of worker's minds, or if there isn't a well-understood policy put in place outlining the security procedures, the punishment is they will be breached. As mentioned before, an Acceptable Usage Policy could help, or something similar mapping out the exact policies and what will occur in the case one of them is broken, as well as whom will carry out these disciplinary actions. It is suggested that in order to maintain an environment of security around the office, that employees be put through an annual training program, visiting both each issue that may arise and how to avoid them. In addition to this program, frequent reminders may be necessary as well, to create security awareness as second nature to any computer user within the office. It is critical that passwords be kept in secure places and not spread around the office.

UPDATING OPERATING SYSTEMS

Often times, the purchase of new operating systems seems like a costly and unnecessary expense, often being put on the end of the priority list for small businesses. In many cases, software for the operating system in use becomes obsolete. This is, however, a huge mistake in terms of cyber security. New operating systems are not only easier to use, more efficient and faster, but each new operating system seeks to improve upon the previous system's security, in terms of having better firewalls and being far less easy to hack or breech.

Though systems like Windows XP or Windows 2003 may seem like they get the job done properly, they are far easier to crash, infect, hack, and steal from, and many times simply because they lack the complexity of earlier models. Operating systems may be renewed by simply installing them on a device of a previous O.S. which is compatible. With this in mind, updating an office full of older computers may not nearly be as costly as having to purchase all new replacement computers. For what you're gaining, renewing computer systems may not be as costly as it is widely known to be.

UPDATING SECURITY PROGRAMS

Similar to number two, old security programs come in as the number three top security concern. Renewing security programs may appear towards the end of a small businesses' priority list, due to both cost and the fact it is generally viewed as an unnecessary expense; however, it is a vital mistake in cyber security as well. Just as in operating systems, security software gets continually more efficient throughout time, working not only faster, but far better technology continues to improve. For this reason, cybercrime easily targets computer systems with obsolete security systems. As if this wasn't bad enough, the actual success of breaches grows with old technology. Fortunately, many subscription security programs come with frequent updates that are absolutely free with the purchase of the system. Consider that; it costs you absolutely nothing to update your security systems! So, why wouldn't you? Well, many business owners and employees do not know how to start these updates or how to check if their systems even need to be updated. This can be easily cured, again for free, with a simple phone call to your security provider's customer service. Their trained, knowledgeable employees will talk you through how to use their programs correctly.

EMAILS AND LOGINS

As previously mentioned, old employees having access to any company emails, logins, or information in general, creates a great security threat that many small businesses are generally uninformed about. Imagine, as an employee who ceased working for a company, how easy it would be to not only use such information for personal gain, but to sell this information to other cybercriminals as well. To ensure that this is a non-issue for your company, discontinue any employee accounts immediately upon termination of their job. This includes email accounts and accounts with access to any customer or company financial information.

In addition to this, it is a great practice, not only for old employees having access to accounts but for cyber security in general, to terminate and renew any passwords to company information every ninety days at the very most. At first this may seem extremely irritating to both you and your employees, but when it becomes a habit it will save you from many breeches that could potentially occur in your business accounts.

PASSWORD UPDATES

Although this may seem painfully obvious and overly mentioned, having any weak passwords is a very serious threat to your cyber security, one of the greatest threats you can easily modify. Although many Americans choose passwords that are the easiest to remember, and even use the same passwords for several programs, this is a great security breech, yet it is also extremely simple to fix.

You may be able to change a password in as little as five to ten minutes, with little to no hassle involved. To begin, keep in mind that the easier the password is to remember, the easier it is to guess as well, and though it may be much less hassle in the short term, being lazy will cost you much, much more grief if your information is breeched. Secondly, avoid any passwords that use a sequence of letters only within the first or second row of a standard keyboard, especially if it is in order from left to right, an example of such being "qwertyuiop."

Never use sports or sports teams as a password. In recent research of popular passwords, well-known sports teams always take their places at the top of the list. In addition to this, any birthdays, first names, or swear words are extremely easily guessable, let alone searchable, and could create a very easy pathway to information, which once is in the hands of cybercriminals, is nearly impossible to get back. Lastly, though it seems blatantly obvious, do not ever use the same password for two or more accounts, it's enough of a burden to have a hacker break into one account, let alone several (or all), because they share the exact same passwords.

EDUCATING EMPLOYEES ABOUT RISKS

Are you not providing information to employees specifically on malware, especially ransomware? What's the first thing that comes to your mind when "cybercrime" is mentioned? Is it a hacker? Or a mass virus? Whatever it may be, chances are it is not malware, which is very concerning, considering that in recent studies malware accounted for the majority of cybercrime that occurred. You may be wondering, what exactly is malware? Malware is quite simply any malicious software, aimed at harming the victim. This is a broader term than you may realize, encompassing any viruses or ransomware, worms, spyware and adware—more generally programs used to obtain private information of a technology user.

Ransomware can come from a number of innocent-sounding vectors, such as an email from your bank or credit union asking for your login information, free downloads, dangerous sites, advertisements, popups, downloads, and even a simple hole in any firewalls. Though some types of malware, such as ransomware or viruses, are very easy to detect, a message may pop up demanding a payment, your computer may crash, work extremely slowly or stop working altogether, yet others are much more insidious, such as spyware, which can live in a computer system for months or even years without being detected. For this reason, malware must be avoided at all costs, which can be done easily through employee education. This may include information on what sites are acceptable to visit, what emails to watch out for, and how to ensure downloads are safe or simply not to download at all.

USAGE POLICY IN PLACE

Similar to both number one and number six, security concern number seven is not having a secure usage policy in place, or a usage policy in place at all. Policies must be upheld through contract and must be signed off on by every employee a company may have. Policies must unfortunately be very specific and often times lengthy for this sort of contract, including what sites a crew member can and cannot visit, download policies, any email policies or secrecy policies for things such as logins or customer information. After employees agree to these policies, there must also be set disciplinary actions in case any employee breaks his or her contract, and whom follows out on these actions. For example, unacceptable usage of company emails will result in a suspension, followed up by a manager and so on.

OFFSITE PROTOCOLS

Many companies don't restrict work to the office, and oftentimes employees may take work home, to public places, or on travel. Security concern number eight is not properly securing devices or logins that are ties to your business outside of the office. When using Wi-Fi, either at home or in public, make it clear to team members they must only connect to secure networks, and some warning signs of private networks is not having a password or having an easy-to-guess password.

Additionally, having a private network with many users such as in an apartment complex, may pose a threat to security as well. Warning signs of public networks is not having users accepting an acceptable usage policy before browsing, or having it not coming from a reliable source.

UPLOAD POLICY

Not disabling automated downloads comes in as number nine, as this is an extremely easy vector for malware to travel throughout. Automated downloads may be automatic downloads when going to a website or opening an email, once downloaded, you cannot fully get rid of whatever the download may have stuck to your device. Disabling automatic downloads is fairly easy, and instructions can be found through a simple google search. Make sure to scan and save any documents you may need prior to downloading them.

LOGGING OFF PROPERLY

The final top security concern for any small business is simply both logging off or out of and closing any system that contains a business' information, especially when using a device at home or a public device in a place such as a library or computer café. When left open, not only criminals, but virtually anybody can steal information from you or your company, making it effortless for them to hack or steal from your business.

It is essential to recognize that serious cyber-security threats abound for SMBs (small to medium-sized businesses). The old saying that "a chain is as strong as its weakest link" has never been truer than in today's constantly changing electronic era. If you need to, explore and secure your protection now – time and hackers wait on no one!

About Larry

Larry Burbano has over sixteen years of experience as an IT expert. He started his IT career when the technology boom was just taking off. Larry pursued studies in the IT field, receiving his Master's from the University of Maryland, with a focus in Cybersecurity. In addition to his formal education, he successfully completed his Bachelors in Computer Engineering and specialized training, receiving certifications that included Security +, CEH, MCP, MCTIP, SharePoint, Microsoft Cloud Integrator, Microsoft Azure Specialist, Certified HIPAA Security Professional, PCI Compliance, and CISSP.

Mr. Burbano is an active, technology-driven person who participates in a diversity of IT conferences nationwide in order to keep up with fast-paced technology advances. He has more than five years of corporate management and enterprise experience. Larry served as a supervisory consultant with the Inter-American Development Bank in Washington, DC, helping to develop and execute their global technology plans.

He has consulted with more than two hundred businesses in the Washington, DC area of varying sizes and industries, and has privately consulted with IT companies in South America. In addition, he serves as a Virtual CIO (vCIO) and successfully designs, implements, and manages automated business, financial, and compliance solutions. He is also the founder of a Cloud surveillance backup and Disaster Recovery Technology company in Colombia, South America, where he helps companies secure their data and video surveillance offsite.

Additionally, he is the co-founder of Play 4 Development, a non-profit organization that fosters youth development projects through sports. Larry devotes his free time to helping kids who are limited to engaging in sports due to a lack of resources in the communities where they live.

Larry is a combination of a super techie and profit-focused entrepreneur. He has been a long-time believer in providing exemplary customer service. His commitment to his clients has been the principal key of his success – he will go all-out providing the perfect solution for his clients.

CHAPTER 5

HOW TO RUN AN EFFECTIVE CYBER SECURITY PROGRAM WITHOUT BREAKING THE BANK

BY ALLEN CASON

Although the names have been changed to protect the innocent. This can happen to you….

It's Monday morning and Sam Soho, CEO of SmallBiz LLC. is going about his daily routine of pouring himself a cup of coffee, logging onto his laptop, and diving into the wave of never ending emails. Just as he is about to respond to his next email, he receives a pop up message on his screen blinking like a neon sign found on the Vegas strip.

The message reads:
ALL OF YOUR FILES HAVE BEEN ENCRYPTED. YOU WILL BE UNABLE TO ACCESS THESE FILES UNLESS YOU PAY A RANSOM IN BITCOINS TO RECEIVE THE NECESSARY DECRYPTION KEY.

First comes shock and then disbelief…

The reality of it all comes crashing in as Sam tries to access just a few of his company's most valuable documents and contacts. . . their client database . . . and the newest client proposal that took hours to create. Each attempt results in a new pop up message telling him that he will only be granted access to this file when he pays the ransom. Grasping his now-pounding head, Sam tries to figure out what to do next as his business grinds to a halt.

Sam then recalled that he had a business card from White Knight IT – a Managed Service Provider (MSP) as the consultant whom he spoke to, called it. If he remembered correctly, they specialized in cyber security issues just like the one he was having. Sam quickly grabbed the old rolodex on his desk that he used to keep his collection of business cards. Sam was old fashioned like that, but this time it just might save his business.

Now holding the card in his hand, Sam could not help thinking that he probably should have called White Knight IT sooner, but he was just so busy. Plus, his business was just a small company of twenty-five employees. . . "Why would anyone bother to target us?"

Sam anxiously dialed the number on the card. A pleasant sounding person answered the phone, "White Knight IT, this is Carolyn... how can we help you today." Sam took a deep breath, as the stress of it all was beginning to overwhelm him. He began to explain his situation to Carolyn who immediately understood that this was an emergency and promptly got Ed, their lead technician, on the line.

Ed explained that Sam's business had been targeted with what is known as CryptoLocker or ransomware, a kind of malware virus used for cyber-crime. He went on to say that this particular virus works by slowly encrypting and then locking access to files on the compromised computer. Ultimately, the ransomware virus encrypts all the files on your computer, making them inaccessible. This has recently become a huge cyber-threat for small businesses, due to the fact that cyber-criminals are now targeting companies where network security is typically far more lax than for larger ones, and where data backups may not be available.

Ed understood that time was of the essence, as this particular virus had the potential to completely cripple Sam's business. Due to the fact that the CryptoLocker virus could continue to propagate across the network and not knowing exactly what or how many files had been compromised, immediate mitigation was called for. Based on his circumstances and given the companies limited IT resources, Ed recommended that Sam begin to isolate the virus by disconnecting any device, wired or wireless, on the network by means of turning off the companies switch as well as their wireless access point (AP).

Ed finished the call by gathering any further information that he might need to mitigate the issue and stated that he would have a technician onsite within the hour.

Once on site, a full cyber-security assessment was completed. It was discovered that the companies main file share server, the data base associated with the company's primary business application as well as Sam's personnel file share which included the all pertinent accounting data had been compromised. In an attempt to restore the data from backup, it was also discovered that the company's differential backup had been run but was found to be corrupted and the last full backup was two weeks old.

In addition, none of the company's workstations, laptops or mobile devices had been backed up. Unfortunately, at this point Sam had some pretty costly decisions to make – either pay the ransom or recover the two-week-old backup and recreate as much of the data possible. Sam just could not bring himself to pay the ransom even if it was the easiest and quickest thing to do to get all of his data back. He decided that he would have White knight IT conduct the two-week-old file restoration and rebuild any infected servers, workstations or laptops found on the network.

Once the storm had past, Sam could not help but to think what he could have done differently given his limited resources. Luckily, White Knight IT was glad to give Sam some recommendations to put in place immediately to run an effective cyber-security program.

COST-EFFECTIVE SOLUTIONS

Based on best practices, from the two leading cyber defense authorities, National Institute of Standards (NIST) and SysAdmn, Audit, Network, and Security (SANS), the following solutions highlight economical and sensible recommendations that can help secure both small to mid-sized businesses (SMBs) networks and critical data.

1. Begin by identifying what data is business-critical to the company's daily operations. This is the data that, if lost, the company could incur significant hardship and costly man hours to recover, as well as substantial loss of revenue and business functionality. Identify all hardware and devices on the network, authorized or unauthorized. The key here is to identify their purpose. Depending on the device that is currently in place (a switch in this case), this can easily be accomplished by conducting a port survey of the switch and the same of the prospective access point.

   With the provided information, you now have the ability to record what each device is being used for and whether not an employee is using all your network bandwidth to view the latest viral YouTube episode of "Kitten's Gone Bad."

2. Software is the next key element of an effective cyber security program. Establish a base line of all software currently being used throughout the network, and then determine what software is needed for each business case. With the use of a freeware tool called Belarc Advisor, an MS Windows product, one can simply build a detailed profile of all software installed on Windows Operating Systems throughout the network.
   Detailed information on this product can be found at:
   http://www.belarc.com/free_download.html

   In addition, a software white list—a listing of all authorized software allowed on the network— should be created. This list should not only include the name of the software package, but its version. An example of this would be Adobe Flash as this software's older versions have been found to be vulnerable to cyber-attacks and one of the sources for CryptoLocker mentioned earlier.

3. Applying secure hardware and software configurations for all servers, workstations and mobile devices on the network is the next key. In most cases, a Windows-based active directory server is present and can easily be configured to globally set group policy across the network. There are, of course, variations; i.e., different operating systems like Red Hat Linux, but for the most part Windows has remained king of the hill. With this in mind, each

server and workstation should be joined to the domain, and every user should be required to have a unique login and password.

4. Password complexity is another important element that can be deployed with active directory and should consist of a unique pass phrase and contain at least a minimum of eight characters but preferably sixteen, including one uppercase letter and one number. The reason for this is that most users tend to write down complex passwords, a major security violation. Password phrases however are easier to remember and tend to be longer in length, and have been proven to lessen the effectiveness of automated password cracking tools.

5. Server access is also a very important consideration. Only designated administrators, usually a primary and back up, should have the ability to login and out and configure the server. This limits configuration capability to the designated individuals.

6. Workstations and Mobile devices also need to be to be deployed with limited access rights and configured with only the intended software to be utilized by each user's job function. The general rule here is that a standard domain user account is sufficient for both devices. Local workstation accounts should be limited to one local administrator for maintenance purposes only. All guest accounts should be renamed and disabled. Workstations need only one network connection, wired or wireless. Any unused and or unnecessary connections should be disabled.

7. All Wireless Access Points or AP's should be secured at a minimum with WI-FI Protected Access II (WPA2) protocol with a pre-shared key (or password) that consists of a pass phrase of at least 16 characters – again including one uppercase letter and one number. Media Access Control (MAC) Filtering should also be utilized to limit access to authorized devices only.

In addition, limit the use of all personnel Mobile devices on the network. Mobile devices can be both a bandwidth-eating behemoth as well as a cyber-criminal's entry point. Imagine that you have the most secure network in the world but then are compromised by a personal mobile device that has been hacked. Ask yourself, "Is it necessary to have every employee able to access the company's network with their personal mobile device?" If the answer is yes, then you are playing with fire and putting your hard-earned business investment at risk.

8. File shares and associated access rights is another key security element. Proper configuration of files shares is often overlooked, but they can can easily be secured by limiting user access to only the file shares that are needed to utilize their job functions. For example, an engineer does not need access to all Human Resources data and vice-versa. Another question to ask is, "Who needs permissions to read or write to the file share in question?" An employee may need "read" access to view his or her own Human Resources data, but the permission to "write" or "over write" the data is not necessary.

9. In regards to email and web browsing: SMBs should utilize Office 365. The entire Microsoft Office Suite is included and provides multiple email features, most notable being email-encryption capabilities. For web browsing, Google Chrome is an excellent choice as it provides a self-updating feature and significant protection from Java and Adobe Flash exploits.

10. Patch Management is also a key security consideration. Within the Windows Operating System, utilize the auto update function which can be set on individual machines, but the recommendation here, based on our scenario, is that it is best to set it up via group policy. The caveat here is that a patch could break a complex third party application—in which case a "back out" of the patch would be required.

11. Backup and recovery. The most economical solutions to date are cloud-based solutions due to the fact they are both automated and require no additional hardware costs. Key features should include strong encryption, file versioning, two-factor authentication, real time backup frequency, adequate storage limits and lastly an easy-to-use user interface.

12. Malware defense should be in place. The recommendation here is SOPHOS with anti-virus and anti-malware functionality.

SOPHOS has a per user license and is relatively easy to deploy. In addition, it utilizes a centralized console for alerting purposes in the event a virus is detected.

13. A firewall is a must for any organization; i.e., Fortinet, Cisco or Palo Alto are at the top of the list. The general rule is to identify and block all unnecessary traffic. The cost effective solution here would be to contact a recommended MSP and work with them to develop a firewall policy that restricts both inbound and outbound traffic to what is specifically required to safeguard your business.

14. Cyber Security Awareness Training is also essential.
Every employee, including management, should be trained to recognize potential cyber security threats. Training should be conducted yearly to encompass any new threats that may have developed. A variety of free materials are available online to help create a Cyber Security Awareness Training program to fit your business needs.

15. An Acceptable Use Policy (AUP) is a necessity. It is not enough for SMBs to just communicate to their employees not to use their work machines for non-work-related activities. It is management's responsibility to create and distribute a written AUP and require all employees to sign off that they have received and read it. For help on designing a policy that's effective, fair, and won't be outdated as your organization expands, SANS has these AUP guidelines. *https://www.sans.org/security-resources/policies/general/pdf/ acceptable-use-policy*

In closing, cyber-threats have increased at an alarming rate. In the last year 8 out of 10 businesses, when surveyed, reported a cyber-security event. SMBs must take heed as cyber-security and cyber-attacks are no longer emerging issues nor do they affect only large companies.

Even more alarming is that ransomware saw a 165 percent increase starting early in 2015. Most recently, a Los Angeles hospital paid a $17,000 ransom in BitCoin to an unknown cyber-criminal to receive the necessary decryption key.

Given the challenges faced by todays SMBs, running and maintaining an effective cyber-security program, in terms of dollars and resources, can seem both a daunting endeavor as well as an expensive one. With limited resources keeping your network secure, it is often likened to trying to bail out your sail boat with a bucket full of holes, all the while trying to stay ahead of the cyber-security storm, looming just over the horizon.

The recommendations here are by no means exhaustive, but only highlight a holistic approach in general, of what a small-to-midsized organization might put in place to weather a cybersecurity storm with a limited budget. Furthermore, each organization has both its own unique requirements as well as legal regulatory obligations, like the Payment Card Industry - Data Security Standard (PCI-DSS) and Health Insurance Portability and Accountability Act (HIPPA).

Using a recommended MSP may not seem like it would be cost effective. But given our scenario, I think you will agree that paying a budget-minded, fixed monthly premium now, is a much better solution than paying later, when it could cost you your business.

About Allen

Allen Cason began his technical career as an "in the trenches" Network Administrator, acquiring his first IT industry certifications while stationed at Quantico, VA, as part of the Inspector-Instructor Staff, 4th Light Armored Reconnaissance Battalion.

Realizing that he had an aptitude for both network operations as well as cyber-security, Allen went on to build a successful 15-plus-year career in the Information Services & Technology sector working for top Fortune 500 companies such as Sprint, EDS and Hewlett Packard. His success stems not only from his experience as a former US Marine but also as an Enterprise Operations Manager supporting and managing one of the largest networks in the world, the Navy Marine Corps Internet.

Allen's passion for cyber-security and his entrepreneurial spirit prompted him to create Strike Point Security – thus establishing his vision for private sector businesses to achieve the same enterprise level support in both network operations as well as cyber security. His company has now grown successfully to become Strike Point Enterprises, encompassing both cyber security as well as managed IT services for businesses.

As CEO of Strike Point Enterprises, Allen is the driving force behind a business dedicated to establishing solid IT solutions for his clients. A firm believer in leadership by example, he leads, trains and motivates his team to be the very best. Due to his innate ability to establish long lasting customer relationships based on trust and dependability, Strike Point Enterprises is recognized as a premier Managed IT Services Provider throughout all of Virginia and the Washington, D.C. area.

Allen is a dedicated family man. He enjoys spending precious time with his wife Carolyn of 22 years and his two beautiful children. He often says... "they are my treasures."

Some of his favorite pastimes include studying History, Science and Archeology. Allen has traveled throughout both Mexico and Central America and was fortunate enough to work with the Texas Christian University on a Mayan archeological dig in Belize. He also enjoys the outdoors and sailing.

Five words you can count on from Allen are: Faith, Integrity, Commitment, Passion and Fun.

CHAPTER 6

SMARTER EMPLOYEES
– TRAINING THOSE YOU RELY ON TO KEEP CYBERCRIMINALS OUT

BY BOB JENNER, The Network Doctor, Inc.

Protecting a company from a cyber-attack starts with employee training. ~ R. Jenner

Many businesses overlook their employees as the main source of protection against cyber-attacks. Employee education is an equally important step to take for businesses to better protect their data and not become a victim of Cybercrime. As a business owner, what do you believe the answer would be if you asked your employees, "What signs do you need to look for to be alerted about a data breach or system attack?" For many businesses, they would receive vague answers from their employees. And why? Because the employees simply do not understand how hackers are relying on them not being informed. That's the way they operate.

Employees touch their employers' technology all day long, both in the workplace and even from remote locations. This includes both the obvious and not-so-obvious things, such as:

- Public Internet
- Business-owned computers
- Employee-owned computers or tablets that are used for business purposes
- Corporate email accounts
- Mobile devices

Giving employees access to their work from all locations can only remain a smart business decision if they understand how to use this access appropriately and safely. It all begins with implementing an Acceptable Use Policy, which will highlight everything that employees must know. Making this a part of the Employee Manual will help employees become more accountable and allow business owners or Information Officers to ensure that the proper training is taking place. Does your business have an Acceptable Use Policy in place? If not, it's time to implement one immediately. You're encouraged to visit the website: www.sans.org to get some free Acceptable Use Policy templates to get you started.

THE SEVEN HOPES OF HACKERS

Think about the big picture of technology. Hackers know all those details and rely on the fact that your employees don't, which makes the "unknowing and uninformed" an ideal source to target for a hacker's own gain. Here are seven things that hackers hope your employees do not know. It's up to you, the business owner, to show them otherwise.

1. Phishing

What is Phishing? Phishing is an attempt to gather sensitive information by email. Two common ways that this information is gained is by making it look like you received an email from either your bank or credit card company that asks you to "update your personal information." You get the email and click on the link and it looks like your bank's website—the only problem is that it isn't. It's a site that hackers have set up to trick you into getting your login information, or possibly worse. Pay attention to the web addresses, consider calling to update information, or else type in the web address yourself so you know that you are at the actual site.

2. Spear Phishing

Spear Phishing differs from Phishing because it is specifically targeted. The attacker may have gathered other specific information about the intended target and in turn, they use this information to lure the target into a false sense of security and get them to divulge information. This can even happen over the phone. Someone may call and say, "We're updating our records and need you to confirm some information." What do you do? You should ask the caller for their extension and call them back. And before you do so, look up the number separately to ensure they actually do work for the company they've indicated.

3. Compromised Website

Websites can be compromised without the owner even knowing it. For example, an attack that was recently out there would tell you that you needed a Flash or Java update in order to see the website's content that you visited. It would then create a popup on your screen with a link to "Update." The only problem is that it did not go to Adobe for Flash or Java.com for Java. It went to the attacker's site and downloaded a Trojan program so that they could remotely take control of and compromise your system. When updating an application like Java or Flash, always go directly to the manufacturer's web site.

4. Compromised Post on Social Media

Social Media is a very easy target for hackers and they tap into it much more than most people would suspect. On average, 600,000 Facebook accounts get compromised each and every day! When this happens, things start to get a little strange on your Facebook pages. Posts you didn't make start showing up, suddenly you are following tons of people you don't even know, spam advertisements are posted to your timeline, and the list goes on. If your business relies on Social Media, this type of invasion can be costly to your reputation.

If I see this, what do I do? First, change your password. I recommend using a commercial password manager program. Programs like these can be used to generate long random passwords that are not easy to guess. The password manager remembers them, so you don't have to. All you have to remember is your one "Master Password." Make that password a good one, using a combination of upper case letters, lower case letters, numbers, and special characters like punctuation. I know, you're wondering, how am I going to remember a password that complex? It's easier than you might imagine. Make a password that is based on an acronym so you can remember it, then change a letter or two. When you do this, a complex password like M#1GfI2$i*! becomes: My Number One Girl Friend Likes to Eat Strawberry Ice Cream! That is a challenging password for even the most persistent hackers to figure out!

5. Lost Cell phone

Most of us would be pretty upset if we lost our phone, just because of the inconvenience, but have you ever thought about the security aspects of a lost phone? If your phone is linked to your corporate email, or you have a VPN client or phone system client that links to your office? How about a file sharing system like Dropbox? If you use your phone for these things you are at risk.

These days, when systems are properly setup, your system administrator has the capability to wipe corporate data off of cellphones and/or tablets when they are lost or stolen. These safety measures need to be implemented before a theft or loss occurs to be effective. Many of the corporate plans from carriers have a "locate" option that can be enabled (for a fee).

6. Lost Laptop or Tablet

Lost or stolen laptops or tablets are even more worrisome than a lost cellphone when it comes to business risk, because they have more storage and thereby can hold more files. There are companies that offer "Lojack for Laptops"; however, this is only effective for recovering lost property back and does nothing to protect data. If part of your job entails the use of what the state calls PII or "Personally Identifiable Information," it is highly recommended to have the laptop hard drive encrypted by your IT department or consultant. Encrypting the data will make it useless to an attacker. The only inconvenience to you is that you will be required to type another password when you start the computer, otherwise it will perform as normal. This is a minimal inconvenience for keeping data safe.

7. Misplaced USB FlashDrive

Have you ever gotten off an airplane after making a business trip and not been able to find the flash drive you were using for those corporate presentations or sales numbers? What would it mean if that fell into the hands of a competitor? Disaster, right? Well it does not have to be that way. There are several companies that make encrypted USB drives. Others make drives that require a fingerprint scan to access. While not as secure as the encrypted models, they at least provide a modest level of security.

These seven things are the most common, but are by no means the only ways that hackers are hacking (or attempting to infiltrate) a business. The only way to give yourself every advantage possible is to ensure that employees are trained in cyber security and the red flags that may signal an attempted attack.

A TRUE STORY

Many attacks come in emails.

Hackers love using email to launch attacks, because they know that it is a lively part of most businesses cultures. Employees check it and are often quick to respond. In the last couple of months, we have seen a new attack that is a very specific and well-worded message by an attacker with inside information. *This specific attack is targeted at larger companies that use ACH or wire transfers to pay vendors.* The email is masterfully crafted, looking like it came directly from the president or a higher-up in the company and it is directed to the Accounts Payable person by name— the one that handles wire transfers. It looks completely legitimate.

This email goes on to reference a vendor that the company uses and provides updated information for a bank account and routing number. Since this is something the company does all of the time, it's not out of the realm of possibility. And most AP people don't want to question an order from the company's president, so what do they do? They send the money.

Since December of 2015, I personally know of three attacks where this has happened. Shockingly, one of the AP clerks actually sent $50,000! How did the attackers do this? They used a sweeping system, which means that the money is pulled and transferred overseas within seconds. It is completely irretrievable. And here's the real shocker: **the banks are not obligated to return these funds!** If the business is fortunate, they have CyberSecurity insurance that can help to mitigate this risk. Nowhere near enough businesses have this insurance, though.

LOCKING HACKERS OUT

Okay Bob, you've succeeded in scaring the snot out of me, what do I do now?

Learning to protect yourself from hackers is something that I help businesses do daily, and nothing pleases me more than when someone asks me how I can help them operate smarter and safer with their technology.

There is no "one thing" that can be done to keep your network safe. **The best approach is to have multiple "layers" of security.** Getting into the technical aspects of a complete security net is more intensive than what a single chapter can cover, but it starts with businesses understanding the basics so they know where to go from there. Use this general information to begin the conversation and actions to make sure your employees and you are doing everything within your control to make your network more secure.

1. External Email Filtering

Have a separate filtering engine in place that goes to work for you before your email server does. Even if you use hosted email like Microsoft Office365, external filtering options are available that exceed what Microsoft offers. These filters stop much of the junk mail, viruses, and spam before it gets to you. A summary of quarantined items is sent on a per user basis several times a day, in case something legitimate gets blocked.

2. Firewall with Unified Threat Management (UTM)

The firewall is the gateway to your network and a professional grade Unified Threat Management system can be built in. UTM has a set of services which includes:

- Policy Based Management
  Policy Based Management allows the firewall to determine what should be allowed into and out of your network by polices that are set by the Systems Administrator, instead of allowing everything and everyone through like consumer devices do.

- Antivirus/Antimalware/Antispam Scanning
  The firewall scans all traffic into and out of the network for viruses and malware. It acts as a "traffic cop," allowing good

traffic (subject to policies) through and blocking bad traffic from entering.

- Web Content Filtering
  Web content filtering controls what your network users can access, including specific types of websites, either by category or by specific user or group, according to your business policies. Users should be given all of the access necessary to do their jobs fully, and no more.

- Application Control
  More than just content filtering alone, application control dictates what applications are allowed to pass the firewall. By doing this, a unique "signature" is attached to each application on your computer. For example: if your business policies don't want to allow access to instant messaging applications they can be blocked at the application level.

- Data Loss Prevention (DLP)
  This is a big one, especially for regulated businesses or those that have specific requirements for the privacy of client information—which is most companies. DLP is a technique where the content going through the firewall is based on a match for patterns. Common examples are for credit card numbers, driver's license numbers, or social security numbers. If the DLP filter detects an email passing through the system with this information, it can block the mail and send an alert to the system administrator, so that the employee can be educated on proper procedures.

3. Centrally Managed Antivirus

Having your computers protected with antivirus and antimalware protection that is constantly updated is an absolute must! Individual applications on multiple computers is hard to manage effectively. Centralized, policy-based management allows for deployment of consistent policies across all of your businesses computers, as well as centralized reporting and alerting.

4. Event Log Monitoring/Management

It's necessary to keep a watchful eye for network problems by looking at the log files. They are a good place to spot hacking attempts, especially if you have terminal or remote desktop servers that are accessible via the Internet without a VPN. These log files also shown erroneous login attempts, which is an indicator of a hacking attempt.

5. Full Image Backups

Full image backups are preferable to traditional file-based backups because they backup everything committed to the disk. This means that open files such as databases are not a problem. Should the worst happen, you can more rapidly recover your entire server.

EDUCATION IS THE FIRST STEP TOWARD PROTECTION

Nothing will protect you if you don't educate your users.

Solid education on preventing system attacks does not have to be complicated. Even something as simple as sharing with employees that they should not click on any email links—YES, none—is effective. If (and only if) they are expecting an email from a business associate should they copy the link into a browser, but make sure the domain is correct, first. Links to videos on YouTube or documents on Microsoft OneDrive can be checked to make sure the links are valid and you're actually going to those sites, and not someplace else.

Remember, hackers are counting on businesses having gaps in employee education. What they don't want you to realize is that you can put up a pretty strong defense against them, and protect your business better as a result.

About Bob

With over 30 years of IT experience, Bob Jenner has watched technology evolve and change our world at a rapid pace. This keen insight into the world of technology and how it impacts businesses—especially small to mid-size companies—has given him expertise that is hard to find.

Prior to working in IT, Bob worked in the electronics industry and also did electronics work within the entertainment industry. But his entrepreneur was calling, and in 1985, Bob started what is now The Network Doctor, Inc. It was a small business that started out as a sole proprietorship and it helped him fully understand the various struggles that most small businesses have. This was valuable information for him to use in order to help others grasp the wonderful potential of technology, while also satisfying his own entrepreneurial spirit.

There are two keys to Bob's success that he values as a person. They are: 1) keeping his word, and 2) integrity. Ensuring these two qualities are a part of everything he touches has helped him develop a reputation as an elite IT source, as well as a guy that is just great to know. Bob's clients can easily identify that he exemplifies his beliefs through his ability to go above and beyond for them. According to Bob, "A client purchased a communication system from my company and it was supposed to have dual power supplies (per the manufacturer claim), but that really wasn't the case. If you pulled the plug on one power supply, the entire system would crash and stop working. I'd given my word that this wouldn't happen. To fix the problem, I took the power supply system home and ended up vesting over 100 hours of my own time to find a solution. And I did it! All of this took place because I gave my client my word and had the integrity to follow through with it."

Bob is the author of the book, *Hassle Free Computer Support,* as well as a co-author of *Easy Prey.* His professional affiliations include: The ASCII Group, Robin Robins Producers Club, Valley Industry Association, and Small/Medium Business Technology Network (SMBTN) and Provisors.

If you were to visit Bob at his office you may be surprised to find a microphone stand next to his desk. Bob has it there because he often does the voice messages/IVR for his client's phone systems. If you've ever wondered about whose voice that is on that phone system, now you know someone who is actually one of those voices. He also enjoys doing voice-over work for fun (both animation and commercial). When other passions aside from technology are calling Bob, he likes spending free time with his wife of nearly 37 years, and they travel frequently. When he's at home, he enjoys being a father to his three grown children, but he's really taken a liking to playing the role of grandfather to his four (and one more on the way) grandchildren.

CHAPTER 7

SECURE BACKUPS
– THE KEY TO MITIGATING A CYBER ATTACK

BY DAVID JORDAN, CISSP, CEH, LPT, GCFE

Cyber attacks can occur at any time and with no advanced warning. 71% of cyber attacks hit companies with 100 or fewer employees.[1] A recent study[2] shows that 9 out of 10 small business owners indicate cybersecurity is a concern. 61% of those surveyed fell victim to a cyber attack within the last 12 months with the average cost of the attack at $36,000. One tool in your arsenal to help you recover your business and mitigate the damage caused by a cyber attack is a rock-solid Backup and Disaster Recovery Plan.

THE THREATS: WHO AND WHY IS SOMEONE OUT TO GET YOU

Hackers are indeed targeting small and medium size businesses. Why would they want to, you ask? Like most people committing crimes, they want to go to where the path of least resistance will be. Given a choice between a Fortune 500 company with a strong cybersecurity posture and lots of security resources or a small business with fewer resources to defend itself with, the hacker will choose the latter. Once your system is compromised there are lucrative things they are interested in doing or obtaining, depending on your business and industry:

- Wiping out data or disabling/destroying systems for the "fun of it"
- Extorting money from you by encrypting your data and systems and then demanding payment in exchange for the password that will decrypt your data (ransomware)
- Stealing personally identifiable information (PII), including social security numbers of employees and clients
- Exfiltrating intellectual property
- Stealing customer information, including credit card numbers
- Taking electronic medical health records of patients or clients
- Gaining access to your banking and financial information

In fact, 19% of companies in the above-referenced study had either their business credit cards and/or their bank account hijacked. This is especially troublesome, as most business bank accounts do not have the same level of protection for asset recovery as what is in place for personal bank accounts.

The easiest way for a hacker to gain access to your company is via your employees. 100% of the time 1 out of 10 people will open an email with a malicious link in it that is sent to them.[3] The best asset in your company are your employees. Unfortunately, they can and usually will unintentionally welcome in a hacker. You must be prepared to deal with the aftermath of a cyber attack and system/data compromise. It is not a matter of "if," but when.

A CAUTIONARY TALE FROM THE TRENCHES: CRYPTOLOCKER - MODERN DAY HIGHWAY ROBBERY!

Unfortunately crime can pay well and CryptoLocker has reportedly grossed up to $30 million in ransom in 100 days![4] CryptoLocker or other types of ransomware are bad news for businesses, but especially bad for businesses that don't backup or inadequately backup, their data.

Ransomware operates by infiltrating your system, typically by tricking an employee via email to click on a link which will download software from a hacker website to your network. From here it "phones home" to get an encryption key and then goes to work encrypting data on your PC and any other system it has access to, including your servers. Imagine all of your word docs, spreadsheets, PowerPoints, photos, PDFs, etc. are suddenly all encrypted and not accessible. At this point it pops up a window on your machines saying you have a limited amount of time to pay a ransom to get the password to decrypt your data. Typically you have to pay $300 - $500 in bitcoin (an untraceable digital currency) to get the password. If you don't have a reliable and recent backup of ALL of your data, you are at the mercy of the digital highway robbers. The thieves typically work on the law of averages and small amounts of money for demand, targeting small-to-medium size companies with fewer than 100 employees. They demand ransom amounts that are small enough not to attract the attention of major law enforcement.

If you follow my advice and have a rock-solid backup you won't have to pay any ransom. Just recover your data and systems from before the attack and you are home-free.

MITIGATE RISKS: BACKUP LIKE YOU MEAN IT!

By properly backing up data, many risks can be mitigated, including that which comes from viruses, ransomeware such as CryptoLocker and its ilk, and data loss due to a compromise of systems or employees. The mitigation comes from the fact that you can restore data and/or information systems to a point that is prior to the attack.

Far too few businesses do not put the proper thought into which data should be backed up and how their data should be backed up. Far too often I hear, "yep, we have a backup" and when pressed for even nominal information about what and how data is backed up, there is a dearth of information forthcoming. There are several factors that can help guide businesses in choosing the proper backup and disaster recovery solution. When a business asks us for assistance in this area, we always start with a few questions and some overall guidance.

First think like a bad guy. This will help you identify and prioritize information systems and assets that need protection. You need to know what you have and where it is in order to protect it.

Second, get advice from a lawyer, IT security consultants and/or industry associations if your company has data that is governed by regulation such as HIPAA or GLBA. This advice also applies if you work in one of several professions, such as legal, finance, or CPA firms, which have ethical obligations to take measures that will hold client data confidential.

Many types of cyber-attacks require notification to the affected parties as well as to governmental agencies. Breach of that data can land you in legal trouble. Furthermore, you may experience a major loss of reputation because the clients/customers that have been impacted by the event may be required to be notified by law, if not by a business's ethical obligation to do so. Knowing all the nuances to your business is important so we can move on to the third step, which is developing an appropriate backup and disaster recovery solution.

The third thing that we evaluate when creating plans for recovering from data loss is to identify the **Recovery Point Objective (RPO)**. In a nutshell, the RPO is: how much data can you afford to lose before it adversely affects your operations? . . . 1 hour? . . . 1 day? . . . 1 week?

A fourth item we look at is what constitutes an acceptable **Recovery Time Objective (RTO)**. How long can a business be without its data or systems before there is a negative impact? How long can you be down? How dependent a business is on information technology and data helps solidify the answer to these questions. In addition, we typically discuss the consequences of losing certain data or systems, as previously identified. What happens when the data and/or systems are gone and cannot be replaced?

What businesses need to think about are the costs of not having a proper data backup and disaster recovery solution for their needs. Even a few days of downtime can be enough to jeopardize a business's livelihood. It is more than inconvenience, you have real costs associated with having your employees unable to do their jobs. There are the hard costs of paying to recover from a data loss or disaster event and there are real soft costs associated with loss of productivity, loss in client confidence, loss of clients, or missing deadlines related to the inability to do your job.

Some sobering statistics:

- 22% of small businesses will experience a data loss that is significant enough to impact their business in some way. This could be loss of revenue, payment of fines or penalties, and/or a damaged reputation.
- 70% of businesses that report a data loss end up going out of business within one year of the event.

If a cyber-attack is the catalyst for data loss and downtime, now is the time to take steps to ensure that you will not become a victim. Having the necessary conversations and delivering information to business owners and decision makers about real consequences of failed technology is something that committed IT professionals do. We have been on the front lines of these events and have experienced, along with our clients, the huge difference that comes from unprepared businesses in comparison to prepared businesses.

PROS AND CONS OF DATA BACKUP OPTIONS

It's natural and expected that a business will want to factor in cost when they are making decisions for what the proper type of backup is for them. It all factors into the RTO and RPO objectives that are laid out for a specific business. Most of the time when review backup and disaster recovery solutions that are in place at most businesses we find that most do not meet the needs of the business. Here are some of the more common types of backup solutions out there with the pros and cons of each:

1. USB, hard drive, and tape:
The most noted 'pro' of this type of backup is cost. It can be a relatively inexpensive way to back up data, compared to other options. However, the 'cons' are substantial, including the following:
There needs to be a manual selection of which data you want to backup, which may change over time if new hard drives are added to systems being backed up. This may lead to a gap in backup coverage. Also, there is the human factor—you must rely on someone to manually change the backup target/media and with tape you will need to have someone periodically clean the tape drive. What happens if it's a holiday weekend or they simply forget? This could turn into a costly error. Many businesses receive email 24/7 and most have remote workers that access/change/update company data files at different times of the day and night. If it is determined that the business has a short RPO then it is only a matter of when, not if, that a business will find themselves in a situation where they've lost vital data. From a RTO perspective it can be extremely time intensive and costly (IT labor) exercise to recover a system or

systems from a disaster. Even if the backup is working you will need to repair/replace the failed system, reload the operating system, rebuild the applications, and get all of the settings on the system exactly right. Only THEN can you restore the data. To give you an idea—using a failed server for this scenario can lead to a full business week of downtime. Manual verification of the backup validity is also required, which means it is almost never done.

2. Internet/Cloud only backup:

A great 'pro' of this type of backup is that it is at least off-site and is typically automated. You can pick and choose the files and folders you want backed up so you know that what you need most is accessible should you have a disaster. The 'cons' are that you must retrieve all of the data over the internet, which can take a long time—it depends on how much you need to restore to return to normal operations. You also need to be aware of adding new locations to backup that you will need to remember, because if they aren't saved in the cloud they are not protected. Most cloud backup solutions will offer to send a disc to you in an emergency, but that does require a payment, and it can be rather costly (averaging $500.00). The RTO issues from the section above also apply. This type of backup typically requires someone to manually test a restore in order to see if what is being backed up is actually recoverable.

3. Appliance based backup data recovery:

This option offers the best of all worlds. There is a backup and disaster recovery (BDR) appliance in your office that takes care of data backup and disaster recovery. These devices back up your systems using an image based backup, a "snapshot," which contains everything on a system, all of the software, all of the data, and all of the settings. It backs up data as often as every 15 minutes and it is done automatically, removing the need for a person to remember to change out the media. This type of solution is what we are likely to recommend to clients looking for a rock-solid backup and disaster recovery solution. We are able to monitor how the system is working on a daily basis, and we do daily tests to validate that what is being backed up can actually be recovered. If a disaster recovery becomes necessary, it can mean business continuity is only interrupted for as little as a few minutes to a few hours, compared to days or weeks.

FIVE STEPS TO BUILDING A ROCK-SOLID DATA BACKUP AND DISASTER RECOVERY PLAN (DRP)

These are the five big things that need to be in place to protect your business data and restore your operations in the event of a cyber-attack:

1. Back up everything with the use of image-based backups to an on-premise device.
2. Encrypt your backups.
3. Send a copy of the on-premise encrypted data to the cloud. It is best to have a geographically separated data center from your office.
4. Test restore data, recovery time, and DRPs often.
5. Have someone be accountable for the process AND the outcome.

When you back up like you mean it, you'll gain peace of mind and proof that if you suffer a cyber-attack you can recover. There is no excuse to not have a working backup solution. We never want customers to experience a disaster, but we are always prepared to help them rebound from one in as efficient a manner as possible.

Footnotes

[1] http://www.wsj.com/articles/how-small-businesses-can-fend-off-hackers-1437088140

[2] http://www.nsba.biz/wp-content/uploads/2015/02/Year-End-Economic-Report-2014.pdf

[3] http://www.inc.com/will-yakowicz/big-business-of-hacking-small-businesses.html

[4] http://www.pcworld.com/article/2082204/crime-pays-very-well-cryptolocker-grosses-up-to-30-million-in-ransom.html

About David

David Jordan is the founder and president of Pacific Computer Consultants (PCC), founded in 2003. David routinely helps his clients align their businesses with technology industry best practices.

Prior to founding PCC David served in many technical roles from companies as large and diverse as Chevron to small local technology businesses as part of the internal IT team. David has more than 22 years in the technical field, the last 13 being an IT consultant and business owner directing a team to deliver complete IT services to small and medium size businesses in the San Francisco Bay Area.

David holds a Bachelor's of Science in Business Administration with a concentration in Entrepreneurship from the University of the Pacific. In addition, he holds the following computer and information security certifications: Microsoft Certified Professional (MCP), Microsoft Certified Systems Engineer (MCSE), Microsoft Small Business Specialist, Cisco Certified Networking Associate, Certified Information Systems Security Professional (CISSP), Certified Ethical Hacker (CEH), GIAC Certified Forensic Examiner (GFCE), and Certified Penetration Tester (CPT).

David's expertise includes: Small Business IT Consulting, Microsoft technologies, network security, virtualization, cloud computing, wireless access, mobile and remote computing, mobile device management, collaborative computing efforts, VOIP Phone Solutions, and backup and disaster recovery solutions.

David has a wife, two daughters and a beagle.

CHAPTER 8

MOBILE DEVICE SECURITY

BY FEMI DADA

Several years ago, one of my clients purchased Apple iPads for all of their employees. This was in the early days of Apple mobile device proliferation, when the use of a mobile device created a real "wow" factor at customer presentations. This particular client worked in the hospitality industry and the ability to use a mobile device to access information and photographs from multiple site locations and events, anywhere, anytime, was a real game changer. Empowering each employee with one of these mobile devices was supposed to improve business agility and provide greater access in order to generate more business.

As the solution provider during the setup of these devices, I raised the concern of ownership, but as is often the case with business owners large and small, this client did not want to burden the staff with any legal agreement or acceptable usage policy. Several months later, a member of the senior sales staff quit and off went the mobile device, loaded with valuable business data and access to all sorts of protected information – such as payroll, marketing, sales, pricing information, and other trade secrets.

With this situation in mind, the question now is how do you secure, manage, and keep all your business data confidential, both at rest and in transit, from that iPad or any mobile device? As a certified security professional and subject matter expert, my goal is to help you understand this emerging, complex world of mobile device security.

WHAT IS MOBILE DEVICE SECURITY AND WHY SHOULD YOU CARE?

It is an undeniable fact that mobile devices (laptops, tablets, smartphones, etc.) will transform your entire business. In today's business environment, mobile devices are serving as the transforming catalyst of an entire way of doing business, both online and offline. You probably have already noticed almost everyone has some kind of mobile device for talking, texting, browsing, social networking, and all sorts of media consumption.

Nowhere is this more apparent than in emerging markets. For example, I am originally from Nigeria and recently went back to visit. Nigeria is considered an emerging, global economic giant in Africa, and the world at large. While I was not surprised, I was amazed to see first-hand how virtually every service delivery, from banking to utilities, occurs on mobile devices and how prevalent Short Message Services (SMS) marketing has become.

Mobile devices are now a worldwide platform of their own, causing organizations to adapt their ways of doing business to fit mobile device platforms. As a business owner or leader, you already operate and use computers in your business and most likely have anti-virus, anti-malware, and other security measures in place. What about your mobile devices? After all, mobile devices are now, if not already, becoming the platform of choice for computing on day-to-day business operations.

The security of mobile devices is all about ensuring safe and secure operation of these devices, when used within any domain of operation. Therefore, taking action to keep data transacted or stored on mobile devices confidential, and ensuring the integrity of that data has not been tampered with, is vital for any mobile device usage, personal or business. The bottom line is mobile devices must be secured to keep your company's reputation and most valuable data, including customer data, trade secrets, intellectual properties, and financial resources, safe and out of the hands of cybercriminals.

UNDERSTANDING RISK POSED BY UNSECURED MOBILE DEVICES

As business owner, your core skill sets are probably not in securing and managing mobile devices or even in IT for that matter. Most likely your focus is on your organization's key goals and objectives, as it should be for any business leader. Unfortunately, because of this we often discover businesses are not aware of the risks unsecured mobile devices pose to the survival of their organization.

You may have heard of a celebrity who lost all their key celebrity contact information to an opportunist at the bar. Why does this matter to your business? Well, imagine losing all your customer CRM data to your competitor because your company uses Sales Force – a Cloud-based CRM which employees can access from mobile devices – and an employee loses their device with unrestricted access to that information, or is terminated and that information is not wiped off their mobile device. What about your financial records in PDF format stored in an email on a mobile device? How about the new strategic partner specifications emailed to you about your company's new product line?

An unsecured mobile device is like a compromised computer left to run 24 hours a day, 7 days a week. A compromised mobile device has unrestricted access to your mobile data plan and can send email, post to social media, and more. A device compromised with a botnet or virus can defame your company's social media site or blast your entire client list with a brand-destroying email in an instant.

To be specific, when an unsecured mobile device becomes compromised it typically leads to the following business risks for the organization:

- Code theft
- External policy violation (HIPAA,PCI, SOX)
- Fraud
- Identity theft
- Information theft
- Intellectual property theft
- Loss of integrity and confidentiality
- Material loss
- Privacy violations
- Reputation damage

MANAGE RISK BY TAKING ACTION

Now that you understand the risk, you must take action to manage it. After all, life and business is about managing risk. Here are some topics to consider when securing your company's mobile devices:

1. **Regulatory Requirements**

   Government agencies and privacy advocates are vigorously making sure privacy rights are not violated. As a result, stringent requirements are being imposed on businesses. Not following these requirements can result in fines, loss of business privileges, and damage to your company's reputation.

2. **Applications Management**

   Managing applications is a critical aspect of securing mobile devices. It involves determining what software can run on the devices and where and how business information is accessed and stored.

3. **Privacy**

   Privacy is a big issue in the U.S., but knowing where the line is drawn is up for debate. When implementing a mobile device security policy, you should have your employees (users) clearly agree the company has absolute access to the mobile device, and can perform a remote wipe to secure company data at any time.

4. **Data Loss and Recovery**

   Defining what data loss means to your business and the procedure to recover it is very important. This also ties into privacy because how information is recovered, accessed, and stored must be defined and agreed upon to fit within privacy requirements.

5. **Labor Laws**

   Various state labor laws define working hours differently, some consider employees answering or checking company email during non-work hours as working and therefore require employers to provide overtime pay. It is wise to check with your state labor laws and put policies in place to ensure employees are not using mobile devices in any way that violates labor laws.

STRATEGIES AND SOLUTIONS TO SECURING MOBILE DEVICES

The good news is there are many solutions and strategies to secure your mobile devices. The challenge lies in deciding which one works best to support your business or organization.

One mobile device security strategy which can prove to be very effective is the Management Approach. With this approach, business managers must come together to set the precedents on security requirements of the business. These requirements then lead to security policies and the policies will drive implementation. The following are ten steps to lead you through the process of implementing a management approach or strategy.

Step 1 – Create a Realistic Policy.

This is the first, and most important step in the journey to securing your business's mobile devices. Your policy will set the goals and objectives of what controls you will need to implement to secure these devices. With the different Operating Systems of mobile devices, it can be quite difficult to setup management for devices on a one-by-one basis. Creating a policy for the use of mobile devices across the board can serve as a meaningful management tool.

Step 2 – Asses your need for a Multi-Platform Mobile Device Security Management (MDM) tool.

Work to determine what kind of mobile devices your business is currently using, including devices from employees who "BYOD" (Bring Your Own Device). Once you know what you are working with, you can then pick what management solution will provide the broadest functions, benefits, and reporting needed to implement your security policies. A good solution will do the following, at minimum:
- Provide visibility
- Offer secure access from anywhere, preferably a Cloud management portal
- Include multi-user access support with read only permissions
- Support local data encryption

Step 3 – Enforce Basic Security. It is critical to do the following:
- Require a strong password.
- Set up device screen lock after a specific period of inactivity (no more than three minutes).
- Enable remote wipe after a certain number of failed login attempts or when a device is reported lost or stolen.
- Enforce local data encryption.

Step 4 – Setup Bluetooth as Hidden or Non-Discoverable.

Disabling Bluetooth helps limit mobile device attack surface from cyber criminals hanging out in close proximity as employees, while still allowing for the user to enable Bluetooth when needed.

Step 5 – Monitor Mobile Device Usage and Policy compliance.

Monitoring devices and reporting on the footprint of those devices provides an inventory of mobile device usage and allows you to respond to emerging threats.

Step 6 – Enable Cost Management for Network Usage.

For example, when this is implemented a global business can monitor and limit international data roaming in an effort to manage costs of mobile devices.

Step 7 – Manage Application Restriction.

This enables a business to limit or restrict applications that are run on mobile devices. It also provides a mechanism to create a "business app store" of apps certified for company usage.

Step 8 – Provide Backup and Recovery.

Ideally, provide the ability to backup data and email and recover it from and to other mobile devices. This works very similar to an iTunes backup of user data and can be specified to allow a business to only backup and recover corporate information.

Step 9 – Limit Data Transfer and Separate Information.

Business can prevent data removal and copying (data leak) from mobile devices. The best practice is to use separation containers to separate corporate data from personal data, prohibiting the mixture of both.

Step 10 – Install Firewall, Anti-Virus, and Intrusion Prevention Solutions.

Yes, mobile devices do have firewalls, anti-virus and other security mechanisms! This security software can be easily installed on mobile devices to ensure maximum security.

Another approach is to hire a Managed Services Provider (MSP) with a specialty in Mobile Device Management (MDM). With this strategy, an

MSP, otherwise known as your IT Support Company or IT guy, manages your company's mobile devices for a predictable monthly fee as part of a management plan for your entire IT infrastructure. This method greatly reduces the risk and worry for your business or organization, and enables the MSP to share the risk by managing the security of your mobile devices. The MSP implements the policy created in collaboration with your organization or business to provide you robust mobile device security.

The third approach to managing mobile device security is the Co-managed Approach. This approach is ideal for larger businesses with internal IT support resources that can manage the policy and day-to-day operations, but leaves the heavy lifting, commonly known as level 3, to the MSP.

If you decide to go with an MSP or a co-managed approach, there are certain things to look for in a provider. Start by finding a provider who works with a policy-based management strategy. In most cases, an MSP that offers MDM will be ready and able to assist a business with crafting a policy. The first step is to set organizational goals regarding mobile device security. This should result in creation of a policy known as a Mobile Device Security Policy (MDSP). It is also sometimes called, or included in, a Mobile Device Use Policy (MDUP). No matter the name, this policy should define and set the tone for using, managing, and securing your company's mobile devices. Once the policy is completed, the MSP can help implement it.

Back to the client mentioned at the beginning of this chapter, remember the company provided employees with mobile devices before putting a mobile device security policy in place, and then lost a device loaded with all sorts of valuable and protected data when an employee left the company. This company has since implemented a mobile device usage and security policy and now has all company data secured, while simultaneously giving access and flexibility to each member of the sales staff. Business data is now kept separate from personal information, company pictures can no longer be downloaded and copied to share with others, and unsecured applications are prohibited. Instead, company certified applications (SecureShareSync) are used to share documents securely with clients and prospects across the world.

About Femi

Femi Dada is a forward-thinking entrepreneur who went into business out of life circumstances, and in the process discovered how to help his clients and customers solve business problems with technology solutions. Femi was born in Nigeria and raised in a family of eleven. At the age of 21, he came to the U.S. on a student exchange program from abroad. Without a college degree, he worked two jobs waiting tables in Washington, DC, and at SunTrust Bank Retail Branch Banking. After his work authorization expired, and with a temporary work authorization, he joined Modis IT as an IT Contractor, where he worked and led various IT support projects, and managed to pay his way through college. He graduated with a B.S. in Computer Science from the University of Maryland University College (UMUC).

While working as an IT Staff Contractor, he discovered inefficiencies in the process of the IT services he was meant to deliver, and as a result, he started Smarthost Design Technologies in 2006. He had the desire to deliver the best in class IT support and technology solution services to help his clients and their businesses reach their full potential. Smarthost Design Technologies has grown in capabilities, including winning an IT services contracting vehicle (GSA IT-70 contract) and securing a government contract to support the U.S. Government Department of Health and Human Services (HHS).

Femi is a leading Subject Matter Expert (SME) in Cloud Computing, Web and Application Hosting, Information Security and Information Technologies Infrastructure Management and Support. He believes that technology is not for technology's sake, but a means to an end in increasing business value and revenue. With his expertise, he serves his clients, businesses, organization and government agencies as a high-level CIO (Chief Information Officer) helping to make good and informed decisions on technologies to support their core business goals, objectives and initiatives. He has been a guest speaker at Young Professional Leadership Group (YPLG), Nigerian-American Information Technology Experts Group (NITEG), and Greater Beltsville Business Association (GBBA) on Cyber Security, Websites That Work, and Technologies to Power Business Success.

He is married to Olga, and together they have a daughter Sophia.

Femi believes that everyone has a God-given potential, and has made it his goal to help others reach theirs – just like he has discovered on his journey here in the U.S. Working in collaboration with clients and a dedicated team of professionals, Femi is looking to solve some of the greatest challenges faced by the world we live in today and solving it with – you guessed it, *Technology.*

You can connect with Femi Dada and Smarthost Design Technologies at:
- femidada@smarthostdesign.com
- www.smarthostdesign.com/easyprey
- www.facebook.com/SHDTech
- www.twitter.com/smarthosttech

CHAPTER 9

MALWARE AND VIRUSES
– DEFENSE IN DEPTH

BY JEFF KUHN

Most people are familiar with the term "virus" as it relates to computers. Viruses have been around since long before the dawn of the Internet. Back then, their primary means of infection were floppy drives. Most of these early viruses were designed to be a nuisance and a headache for those who were infected. Once the Internet came along and became more mainstream, the methods by which a computer could be infected rapidly expanded. As the means of infection have expanded, so has the purpose of infection.

I experienced this firsthand with a company that reached out for help several years ago. They were a plumbing supply company who had thin margins on the products they sold. We were brought in to help identify why a number of computers in their office had been running extremely slow for quite some time. After running Antivirus and Antimalware scans, it turned out the computers were infected with a piece of commercially available software. This software was logging all their keystrokes, gathering data, and emailing it off to an unknown third party. It would also take any email sent by the unsuspecting user and send a copy to the unknown third party. We were able to trace the infection back to an email with an attachment that silently downloaded and installed the malware on the infected computers, which meant each infected machine was now sending the keystrokes and emails to the third party. We were able to remove the malware, but the damage had already been done. The company had suspicions the infection was the act of a rival company. Within six months, the company we tried to help went out of business. It was simply too late.

The rise of online banking, E-Commerce, and other Internet-based financial tools has transformed Malware and Viruses from tools used to annoy to tools used to generate profits. Malware is no longer used as a prank, like the stereotypical teenager "Hacker" in a basement trying to infect computers to have a good laugh. Malware today is created, used, and sold by organized criminal enterprises. These criminals typically tout their wares on the "Dark Web," an underground network that exists on the Internet, but can only be accessed via special proxy software or authentication, such as Tor. The criminals providing the software for purchase also provide help desk support, money-back guarantees, and how-to guides on how to profit from its use.

My company recently had a company call us in a panic because they were unable to open the files on their server and hoped we could help. When they attempted to open up documents, they would receive an error that the file was corrupt. When we arrived onsite, we determined they had been hit with CryptoLocker malware, a common type of Ransomware. Ransomware is a piece of malware typically delivered via email with an infected attachment claiming to be an "unpaid invoice" or "shipment tracking" in PDF or Word form. While investigating, we tracked down the point of infection to a single employee. The employee, who typically handles package shipments at the company, received an email with a PDF file attached posing as a package tracking document.

When the user opened this attachment, it silently installed the ransomware malware. The malware then proceeded to find all the documents (Word, Excel, PowerPoint, PDFs, etc.) on his local computer, as well the documents on the server this employee had access to, and encrypted them. This encryption makes all files unreadable unless you have access to the decryption key. The criminals left a message on the user's PC that the files had been encrypted, and in order to receive the decryption key, they must pay a ransom using BitCoin within a certain amount of time. If this was not done, all the files would be encrypted forever.

Once this happens, the only way to recover the files is to either restore the files from a previous backup or to pay the Ransom. When we inquired about their backups, they said they "thought they had a backup." Looking through the backups, it had not run in over a year. This left them with the only choice of paying the $300 ransom to get their files back, without losing a year's worth of work, and hope the criminals sent the decryption keys. In this case, they were lucky and their files were restored. This unfortunate situation could have easily been avoided if the company simply had appropriate IT security measures in place.

The bottom line is that cyber criminals use a vast array of methods to attack networks and devices, followed by numerous methods in which your information is used criminally. There is no one foolproof method to block everything. Rather, the best bet is to have multiple strategies in place to secure your network. Implementing layers of security is the best way to prevent infection. You must create a defense in-depth strategy.

PROTECTION AT THE PERIMETER

The first layer of security to protect your network is to create a wall of protection around the perimeter by implementing a firewall. Keep in mind that not all firewalls are created equal. The combination modem/ router that is provided by your Internet Service Provider adds little in the way of protecting against advanced threats. The way we protect clients is by installing a Next Generation Firewall (NGFW). A NGFW adds intelligence to the Firewall, by implementing several key features including antivirus scanning, content filtering, application blocking, intrusion protection, virtual private networks, and geographic restrictions.

Antivirus Scanning is a well-known step which simply entails scanning traffic before it hits the user's browser. Content filtering is blocking access to risky sites, such as gambling sites, while application blocking applies to blocking risky applications, such as peer-to-peer downloading sites and proxies, both of which are more likely to infect your network. Tor is an anonymous network proxy that can create anonymity and attempt to bypass firewall rules. Some malware, such as the CryptoLocker ransomware uses Tor for communication, so blocking access to Tor and proxy software is a must. It is also a good practice to put geographic restrictions into place. Certain countries are known to be riskier to communicate with because of the large amount of viruses and malware that originate from them. If there is no reason to communicate with these countries, it is wise to block communication with them.

The key to successfully protecting the perimeter is to engage with an IT services firm that can conduct a security audit and recommend the best NGFW to fit your needs. Also keep in mind, simply installing and configuring the device is not enough for adequate protection. The NGFW should be updated frequently, monitored for possible breaches, and tested to ensure it is protecting your network to the fullest.

ANTI-VIRUS AND ANTI-MALWARE

Installing and actively managing anti-malware and anti-virus programs on all company devices and servers is a must. It is a tool recommended as a best practice for any business. These programs should be locally installed on computers, phones, etc., and centrally controlled, with built-in reporting to alert IT of attacks. The best anti-virus programs not only block viruses, but removes them and alerts users and administrators, so proper follow-up and remediation can take place. A centrally-managed and actively monitored anti-virus solution ensures each computing endpoint is up to date with the latest virus and malware definitions and allows visibility into which endpoints have encountered an infection. It is helpful to choose an IT provider that provides 24/7 monitoring and can provide immediate remediation should a threat be detected.

EMAIL SPAM AND VIRUS FILTERING

SPAM and Phishing emails are a common way companies become infected with Malware. This may come in the form of an email requesting you click a link to verify your banking details, or with an infected attachment criminals hope you open to let the malware install on your device. A best practice recommendation is to route your email through an antispam service that will scan for viruses and protect you from incoming email threats. Most of these antispam services not only provide antispam and virus filtering, but also allow you to encrypt outgoing email to protect emails with sensitive data from prying eyes.

PATCHING AND UPDATES

A popular attack method used by cyber-criminals is to hack legitimate websites and infect them with Malware. In fact, over 80% of all websites infected with malware are legitimate websites. When users access these websites, Malware is silently downloaded, and the malware is able to detect known vulnerabilities in your operating system, browser, or other third party application like Java or Silverlight using a piece of software called an exploit kit. Once it finds an exploit to gain access to your system, it downloads additional malware to steal your data. In order to defend against these attacks, which are referred to as drive-by downloads, the best protection is to keep your operating system and applications patched with the latest updates. A key to this protection is monitoring and reporting on patches. A qualified IT services firm will help you put a system in place where patches are delivered automatically to your devices as needed. Monitoring the patch status of these devices is key to closing any holes that might exist in your operating system or applications.

MOBILE DEVICE MANAGEMENT (MDM)

Mobile devices should not be forgotten when planning your defense strategy against malware and viruses. Cell phones and tablets can get infected just as easily as a computer can, and this can in turn infect your corporate network. In fact, most mobile phones are used outside of the corporate network, where users access their own home Wi-Fi networks and guest wireless networks in hotels and restaurants. MDM tools provide anti-malware applications and monitoring so companies can keep the corporate network safe when mobile devices are used.

BACKUPS

Most of the time companies have a backup procedure in place. The problem that most often arises is that backups are not monitored for success or failures on a consistent basis. Do you know when your backup did not compete successfully? If your files were encrypted with Ransomware malware, would you be able to successfully restore those files? If you could restore them, how long would it take? Minutes, hours, days? These are all things that must be considered when creating a backup strategy. There are numerous backup solutions on the market, the newest of which is an appliance with the ability to backup files as often as every 15 minutes. In the case of a disaster or malware outbreak, the restores can occur in a matter of minutes, as opposed to other solutions which could take days. The key to having a rock-solid backup strategy is to implement a solution which alerts you of successes and failures, can restore files quickly and easily, and tests your backups on a regular basis. Even if your daily backup report indicates all is well, testing is the only definitive way to make sure that when a restore is needed, it will work correctly.

REMOTE USERS

When users connect to the corporate network from elsewhere a VPN (Virtual Private Network) should be used, every time. VPN is an encrypted, and therefore much safer, connection to the network. It can route web traffic through the corporate office, so users are protected by the same firewall as if they were in the office. A VPN will utilize the company firewall to ensure corporate policy is followed, thus helping protect the company.

LEAST PRIVILEGE

There is no reason to give a user greater access to your network than necessary. When we first engage with a new client and perform a security audit of their network, we find many users have administrative rights on their computers. While this adds the convenience of users being able to install their own software, it also increases the attack surface and makes the attackers jobs more convenient. The same applies to granting users access to data on the server. Only provide access to data that is required for them to carry out their job. Taking this action makes it harder for malware to be successful and helps keep your network more secure.

EDUCATION

The final, and one the most important steps, in a defense in depth strategy is to educate your employees and users. One specific action is to put an AUP (Acceptable Use Policy) in place. An AUP outlines what a user is allowed to do on the corporate network. Users must accept, or sign it, before being able to use your network. In addition to taking tangible steps toward user education, it is very important to create a culture of security. You must teach employees to always think about security. Take the steps to ensure if they have a question about an email, think a website is risky, or receive a popup they will tell someone. To do this, you must conduct security awareness training a few times a year.

This type of training will answer employees questions such as, "I got an email attachment. Should I open it?" Or, "If someone calls claiming to be from IT and is requesting my password, should I give it?" While the answer may seem obvious, it isn't to everyone. A common tactic used by hackers and cyber criminals is Social Engineering. Cyber criminals employing social engineering will pose as an employee of your company, or someone who just needs to "confirm your identity" by asking for your personal or financial information.

Another social engineering tactic that has been widely used is to leave a USB flash drive in the parking lot or other public place in hope that someone will pick it up and plug it in to their PC. This USB drive ends up being infected with Malware, and just by plugging it into your PC you have granted the hacker access to your corporate network. The U.S. Department of Homeland Security conducted a study on the effectiveness of this method by dropping USBs and CDs in the parking lots of government employees and private contractors. 60% of the people who picked them up plugged the devices into office computers. A CD or USB with an official logo on it was likely to be plugged in by 90% of people who picked it up!

While there is a lot of work to be done to protect your business from malware and viruses, it is completely feasible for any business to do so effectively. One of the easiest ways to protect your business is it to hire an experienced IT firm or consultant, with strong experience in cyber security, to help you. In whatever manner you get the work of protecting your business from cyber threats done, be sure you include all the strategies discussed in the chapter. Create a defense in-depth strategy!

About Jeff

Jeff Kuhn is a Senior Solutions Architect and Partner at New England IT Partners, an IT Managed Services company serving clients across New Hampshire and Massachusetts. He has over a decade of experience working in the IT field. Prior to New England IT Partners, Jeff worked as a Software Performance Engineer for a Fortune 1000 company. He also was a Senior Sales Engineer for an enterprise software company where he was responsible for implementing software solutions at large companies across the globe.

Jeff has a broad range of IT skills, and his specialties include Virtualization, Backup and Disaster Recovery, implementing cloud solutions and security. In Jeff's current role, he works closely with small to medium-sized businesses (SMBs), to help them implement technology solutions that meet their business needs. In addition to lightning fast response time and customer satisfaction, the proactive solutions of New England IT Partners ensure that companies can focus on their business, and not worry about IT.

Jeff holds a Bachelor's degree in Business from Saint Anselm College, and enjoys spending time with his wife and three kids, as well as playing hockey and enjoying the outdoors.

CHAPTER 10

MID-TIER BUSINESSES MUST EMBRACE THE CLOUD IN THIS CYBER-HACKED WORLD

BY GREG HANNA

Hurricane Sandy may go down as one of the worst disasters in history. It was the largest hurricane of 2012 and second-costliest U.S. hurricane ever. It created a huge path of destruction and left nearly half a million people without power.

Many businesses were among those left powerless during the aftermath of Hurricane Sandy. One of those was a law-firm that lost power for a week-and-a-half after the storm. Thankfully, the firm had just implemented a full Cloud solution, which put 100% of the company's IT securely into the Cloud. While the office was closed due to the power outage, the firm was as productive as normal because all employees were able to work remotely, securely and seamlessly, mostly from the comfort of their own home. The managing partner was even able to work from a Starbucks close to the office, in case he needed to get to the paper files. If this firm had not been fully integrated into the Cloud, it would have suffered major financial losses like most companies in New England and New York were experiencing due to Hurricane Sandy.

WHY THE CLOUD?

Computer/mainframe sharing from a centralized, highly-secure and redundant facility is not a new concept. IBM began this model in the late 1950's with mainframe time-sharing speaking to teletype terminals. In the 1980's and 90's every company in the world began to embrace the personal computer and built their own in-house "datacenters" and computer resource sharing via local-area and wide-area networking. As internal demands increased and computer access became a lifeline for all companies, small-to-medium enterprises (SME) began spending hundreds of thousands of dollars on equipment and man-power to support and maintain an IT beast that could not be tamed. Fast forward to 2010, businesses finally woke up and realized the IT "companies" they had built within their organizations were costing a fortune. In comes the Cloud, eliminating the need for in-house and outsourced IT services and allowing companies to focus on their core purpose, which is generally not IT.

BENEFITS OF THE CLOUD

Through use of the Cloud, a company can take full advantage of millions and millions of dollars' worth of hardware, software, and services, without having to own any of it. This unparalleled access levels the technology playing field across business of all sizes, enabling an SME with fifty users or more to enjoy the benefits of Fortune 100-level computing resources and services, while actually saving money in the process.

In addition to disaster protection and greater access to resources, the Cloud provides businesses with virtually limitless capacity and storage and a system that never goes out of date and is always maintained. It also serves as a very strong defense against cyber-crime. Use of the Cloud keeps businesses focused on business, instead of being slowed down by needs for greater capacity, speed, protection, and technology upgrades. The Cloud frees a company from the never-ending technology hardware and software re-fresh cycle, while at the same time providing enterprise-level logistics, processes, and world-class 24/7 service and support.

THREE WAYS COMPANIES CAN TAKE ADVANTAGE OF THE CLOUD

- **The Private Cloud**
  This is a system a company hosts internally from its own data

centers or rents from an outside hosting company, through the use of an isolated, dedicated infrastructure. The advantages of the Private Cloud are it uses a business's internal assets, provides greater physical control, and offers a sense of security. The disadvantages are that this is the most expensive option, requiring a company to hire internal or external specialists to manage, fix, upgrade, and maintain it. If disaster recovery and business continuity are desired it is necessary to invest in two separate locations, doubling your investment. Security should be managed full-time. While this method can provide a sense of being secure, it usually is a false sense of security. The problem is the security for these systems is typically only a single firewall appliance and some intrusion detection and prevention appliance or software added-on to the firewall itself.

- **The Hybrid Cloud**

  With this option, the company keeps some technology and services internal and hosts other services with a Cloud provider, generally a public Cloud provider to keep the costs down. An example of Hybrid Cloud is outsourcing the email system (Microsoft Exchange for example) to a Cloud Provider and keeping everything else internally. On the positive side, this creates all the Cloud advantages for the app(s) put into the Cloud, reduces total cost of ownership, and creates a decent ROI, for the Cloud apps. Negatively, all the apps left internally experience the same problems found in a Private Cloud setup.

- **The Public Cloud**

  This option is the most advantageous to a company. Financially, it eliminates capital expenditure investments every three to five years for new servers, software, storage, and services. The Public Cloud offers dramatic flexibility. Need ten users? They can be turned on in under 10 minutes. Laying off fifty users? Turn them off and save 50 times your monthly cost per user. More storage, better security, up to date Microsoft Office, and 24/7 support are all included.

ELEVEN REASONS WHY SMALL-TO-MEDIUM ENTERPRISES MUST MOVE TO THE CLOUD NOW

As a business leader, you probably only think about IT when there is an immediate problem. That's not unusual. However, more and more companies are recognizing the IT system they have in place is not capable of providing the benefits they need at affordable prices. Ask yourself, have your investments in IT provided your company the following benefits?

- Anytime, anywhere, any-device access
- Budget predictability
- Consistently good user experience
- Disaster recovery
- Proven and testable business continuity
- Robust cybersecurity

If not, it is time to join the Cloud revolution and allow your company to concentrate on your core business. Consider these eleven reasons to move to the Cloud:

1. **Lowered IT Costs:** This is probably the single most compelling reason why companies choose to move their company to the Cloud. Companies I've worked with have realized savings from 20% to 52% when moving some or all of their IT to the Cloud. These savings come from reduced or completely removed costs associated with the following:
   - Hardware (servers, storage, laptops, and workstations)
   - In-house IT support and/or outsourced IT consulting
   - Software licensing
   - Upgrades

   Once a company moves to the Cloud, it no longer needs to write large checks every one, three, and five years. Capital expenditures disappear and are replaced with much lower costs and higher ROI operating expenditures. With the Cloud you only pay for what you need, when you need it.

2. **Savings on Capital, Staffing, and Services:** Once a company moves to the Cloud, it no longer has to spend tens or hundreds of thousands of dollars on servers, storage, operating systems, and infrastructure, all of which are generally obsolete within 6-12 months of purchase. A company no longer has to install, update, and maintain software and support the system overall. This is particularly attractive for companies who are wasting a lot of money on external IT services and/or internal IT staff. Companies that are new, expanding, or facing a major IT upgrade, and don't want to incur the heavy outlay of cash required for purchasing

and supporting an expensive computer network will benefit from The Cloud. The Cloud takes the variable capital, operating, and human resource expenses off the income statement and replaces them with a predictable, scalable, single line-item under monthly utility expenses.

3. **Advanced Cybersecurity:** Cloud platforms are far more robust and secure than your business network, because they utilize economies of scale to invest heavily in security, redundancy, and failover systems making them far less likely to go offline. Instead of a single or several cyber-threat prevention devices, the Cloud uses redundant clusters of these devices, which are constantly monitored and fine-tuned to thwart threats. If you lost your password today, or if your employees share passwords and someone leaves, your company is vulnerable. Cloud systems use 2-factor authentication (2FA), which protects your company from lost passwords, easy passwords, and hacked accounts. For example, with 2FA, after you enter your password you need to accept a connection request on your mobile device that is unique to you and changes every 60 seconds. Cloud companies' have many clusters of firewalls, IDS and IPS systems, a Security Operations Center (SOC), and use Security Information and Event Management (SEIM) technology to create actionable items from terabytes of security log data. Cybersecurity is part of a quality Cloud service and is done on a massive, industrial grade scale.

4. **Instant Encryption:** Although data encryption is critical, it is a mystery to most. Internally managing devices, SSL certificates, and multiple pathways to information is a nightmare. Thankfully, Cloud platforms eliminate these issues. All data is encrypted in-flight (when traveling from one computer or one site to another) and at rest. These are both important as unencrypted in-flight data can be captured in clear-text format and data at rest can be hacked or physically stolen by taking the drives, servers, or devices. Given the option, it's worth every penny to add-on both email encryption and whole disk encryption. Email encryption will automatically protect your company from damages when an employee accidentally sends personally identifiable information or confidential information to a third party. Whole disk encryption will protect your company from significant damages that arise

when something, even seemingly simple, happens. For example, a company with 75 employees recently had to pay millions of dollars in damages and credit monitoring for the "potential" disclosure of records when one of their employees left their laptop at a bar after a Friday happy hour. Within a year, the company had less than 10 employees on staff.

5. **24/7 Data Security:** Let's suppose the data your applications are accessing and the documents you are writing never "leave" the data center. It looks as if the documents and databases are physically installed on your PC, but they're not. A huge advantage of a well delivered cloud system is that your applications and documents are usable at lightning speed (sometimes even faster than if installed locally) and are all safe and secure in the Cloud data center away from hackers, harm, and theft.

6. **Compliance:** Another significant benefit the Cloud offers is the ability to mostly or entirely handle a company's IT and data security compliance requirements by simply being in the Cloud. Cyber-crime is growing exponentially and federal regulations imposed on healthcare, financial, and insurance institutions are driving billions of dollars into regulatory compliance requirements for businesses who work with or in these regulated industries. HIPAA, SOX, and PCI are just a few compliance challenges facing businesses. Each of these compliance audits and certifications cost between $25,000 and $65,000 annually, and for larger companies those costs increase by factors of 10 and 100, respectively. The good news is all reputable Cloud companies undergo these same audits. The benefit to you, if your IT is in the Cloud with a compliant Cloud provider, is that your company can "ride" on the compliance certifications of your Cloud provider for those areas relevant to your IT compliance.

7. **Automatic Disaster Recovery and Backup:** The servers in your office or data center are extremely vulnerable to a number of threats including viruses, human error, hardware failure, software corruption, power outage, and physical damage from fire, flood, or other natural disaster. In the Cloud, your office or data center could be totally unavailable and all you would need to do is grab a laptop or mobile device and you'll be back up and running

immediately. This would NOT be the case if you had a traditional in-house network and were using tape drives, CDs, USB drives, online backup services, or standard disk-to-disk devices to back up your system.

8. **Enhanced Business Agility:** The Cloud makes any-sized business agile. It makes setting up new employees faster, cheaper, and easier. If a company uses a seasonal workforce or has a lot of turnover, Cloud computing will not only lower the costs of setting up new accounts and having elastic licensing costs, but it will make it infinitely faster.

For example, my company currently provides the Cloud platform for a local firm that brings on an average of 10 summer interns each year. With a traditional network setup, they would have to purchase expensive PCs and software licenses for these temporary workers and then pay to maintain and upgrade them throughout the year. Using Cloud computing, these interns use their own laptops and log into the network securely. The firm ONLY pays for those workers' licenses during the time when they are interning. When September comes around, the firm no longer pays for those licenses and support used by the summer interns. Using this model saves the firm approximately $27,000 a year in hardware, software, and IT services.

9. **Improved Employee Productivity:** In today's always connected society, if you make it easy for an employee to work from their favorite mobile device, they will, no matter what day of the week or time of day. This drives increased revenue, profitability, and customer satisfaction. Cloud computing takes the mobility out of the specific device and inserts it into the user. In other words, it's not the device that's mobile, it's the user. This makes which device an employee chooses to use, and from where they choose to use it, irrelevant. Any device, anytime, anywhere is truly flexible and mobile.

10. **Reduced Real Estate Costs:** The Cloud is an offsite system that will save on real-estate costs. Real-estate is expensive and with the economy turning around, the cost per square foot won't be coming down any time soon. Smaller companies can reclaim the

server room and companies who own and rent data centers can save tens of thousands per month.

11. **Greener Technology:** The Cloud is a greener technology that will save a business on its electric bill. For some smaller companies, the power savings may be too small to measure. However, a larger company with a datacenter or server room can realize considerable savings by no longer having to cool a server room and keep the servers running 24/7. One of our clients had four cabinets of servers and storage costing them an average of $5,700.00 per month for power and cooling. This cost was eliminated when they moved to the Cloud.

SUMMING IT UP

There must be a reason both IBM and HP have stepped away from selling servers to the SME marketplace. The reason is simple. There is a dramatic and disruptive shift in the technology of how businesses will consume IT. The shift has already begun and will explode through its momentum phase over the next five to seven years. Companies have finally begun to wake up and realize they need to focus solely on their product or service to be profitable. IT is an expensive distraction. Companies are moving, and will continue to move 100% of their IT apps, servers, storage, and services out of their company and into the Cloud. If your company hasn't already, now is the time to move to the Cloud.

About Greg

Greg Hanna is an entrepreneur, speaker, best-selling author, and seasoned business executive. Leveraging his 30 years of industry experience, Greg helps CEO's, Presidents, and owners apply the appropriate blend of security, reliability, performance and savings to their IT system, enabling them to achieve their critical business initiatives. Greg has a long history of identifying, developing and launching leading-edge technology services, years ahead of industry adoption.

Greg is currently the President and CEO of TOSS Corporation, the IT industry's most in-demand Cloud computing company specializing in highly effective technology strategies bringing true efficiency, agility, and increased productivity to U.S. based businesses. He is a graduate of the University of Rochester, and his business passion is helping companies get out of the technology business by providing them with his IT as a Utility® platform, which is an enterprise-class Cloud delivered IT system complete with provisioning portal, cybersecurity, and 24/7 service and support. Greg's customer service philosophy is, "If each client feels like they are the only TOSS client, we've succeeded."

Greg is the author of Computers Should Just Work! He has been featured in many publications including The National Law Journal, Journal of Investment Compliance, Cybercrime: Current Perspectives, and has been a featured speaker at numerous ALA, ILTA and other Legal, Healthcare and IT events and conferences.

You can find Greg at:
- Greg.Hanna@TOSS.net
- www.Twitter.com/GregHannaCEO
- www.linkedin.com/in/GregHannaCEO

CHAPTER 11

HOW TO MANAGE SECURITY IN A CLOUD-BASED WORLD

BY MATT KATZER, KAMIND IT

Many business owners believe that because we now exist in a Cloud-based world, we need to change the way we manage security. This is not strictly true. The same rules we use, or should be using, to manage security for our current on-premises environment are the same as the rules that should be in place for using the Cloud to conduct business.

What has changed, exactly? And why is the way we managed systems in the past different from what it is today? We can put this into perspective by looking back at the history of cyber attacks, which had three phases (See Figure 1). In the early days cyber attacks started out harmless enough—we had to protect our businesses from mischief attacks. But when mischief was no longer satisfying to the attacker, they upped their game and it became one of theft, which was often run by organized crime. Now, as we look into the future, the "big threat" to businesses is that of funded state-sponsored attacks.

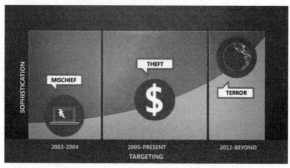

Figure 1. Lifetime of Cyberattacks (Courtesy of Microsoft)

Fundamentally, nothing has changed from a business owner's perspective. We still are faced with the same problem. The difference comes from the type of attack, as they are now much more organized and designed to penetrate networks to access business information. It's through looking at attacks today that we can see that when an entity wants to break into our environment, they do research on us—just as much as we'd do when hiring a new employee. This results in a huge problem because more often than not, we have not increased our vigilance, nor changed our business methodology.

BUSINESS INFORMATION HAS BECOME MORE FLUID

Business information has become more fluid with the increase of technology. In turn, this has created a significant problem for business owners. Now, the attackers are more sophisticated. And on the business side, in order to grow and adapt to new ways to work, we have become more mobile and free with the information that we communicate and supply.

As an example, let's look at the development of a business proposal in a different language. Typically, how is that document translated? Most people will look for free tools on the web to translate the document from one language to another. They don't even bother to evaluate the cost of the tool. And realistically, free tools appear to be just that—free. However, they do require the users to supply proprietary business information in exchange for using the tool. There is no financial exchange, but an information exchange. However, consider this question: do the employees give any consideration about what happens to the raw data? Likely not, but rest assured, it is not being requested for no reason. That information is being sold.

In Figure 2, we see the four common ways in which business information is leaked to the external world. Some are a lack of human judgment and some are through data breaches. We are looking at exposure due to: the use of mobile devices; employee access to social media sites for collaboration; documents emailed to third parties; and, data breaches that go undetected in the network.

Figure 2. Typical security leaks in our business (Courtesy of Microsoft)

Looking at who is trying to penetrate our networks, and the methodologies that we have in place, it is clear that we need to change. We need to develop different ways to protect ourselves and our business.

Today's environment has changed. The tools we rely on are now machine learning-based. In Figure 3, we can view an example of software that runs inside your network and reviews the different activity of your on-site users and Cloud users. The purpose of this software is to provide an early warning that indicates possible network penetration. How does this work? If you have a user who routinely accesses the shared file server for presentations and now that same user accesses the accounting records, you need to be able to detect that and stop the network penetration. These types of behaviors are all indicators of potentially suspect activity.

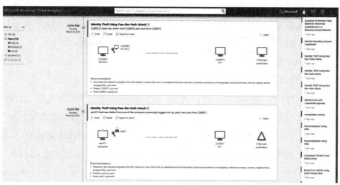

Figure 3. Machine learning detection example (Courtesy of Microsoft)

WHAT SHOULD BUSINESSES DO TO PROTECT THEMSELVES?

Businesses are built on trust, however, trust sometimes is not enough. To assist in the management of your environment, we have a set of rules to follow when looking at SaaS (Software as a Service) applications and the business' security needs. These rules work with most SaaS Cloud vendors, but specifically we use these rules to vet Microsoft cloud services.

These are the ten security questions that you should definitely ask a Cloud supplier:

1. Is the Cloud solution HIPAA compliant? Any business that is regulated by HIPAA needs to make sure they are doing their due diligence to protect PII (Personally Identifiable Information).
2. Does the Cloud solution include data loss prevention tools? You want to have image back-up and be able to restore all lost data, regardless of a breach or a system failure.
3. Does the Cloud solution use two-factor authentication to reset the password? This is a highly effective step in preventing data theft and financial theft.
4. Does the Cloud solution use machine learning? Patterns and behaviors of an employee or organization can be identified, helping to further ensure security.
5. Does the Cloud solution provide integrated security with on-premises equipment?
6. Does the Cloud solution allow you into extended security credentials of the hosted service?
7. Does the Cloud solution provide monitoring tools for security? Logs, records, and notation of all activity on the network makes it easier to identify attackers, as well as human error.
8. Does the Cloud solution allow you to force authentication verification for breaches?
9. Do you have an on-site SaaS monitoring solution that provides early threat detection? Hackers seldom gain entry on the first attempt. With the right software, you can detect when someone is trying to enter into your system that should not be there.
10. Does the Cloud solution monitor security breaches by looking at accounts for sale on the open market? There is an Internet black market for criminals, where they can find buyers of stolen information. Your Cloud monitoring service should monitor this activity.

The issues for all businesses in a Cloud world are simple: how do we increase the productivity of the users and how do we protect company information? Looking at the employees in our work force, statistically 93% of the workers admit to violation of corporate data protection rules, while 80% of workers will admit that they routinely download un-approved software. Most of this activity is unknown to the business owner or on-site IT staff. Learning how to recognize and monitor all activity on the Cloud and on networks is necessary. From my professional experience, Office 365 and EMS Management Security offer options that can meet the demands and needs of business' technology and networks.

HOW OFFICE 365 AND EMS MANAGE SECURITY

Office 365 is a suite of technologies delivered as a Cloud SaaS offering. Office 365 reduces the IT costs for businesses of any size and significantly reduces the need for an IT professional to manage the Office 365 services.

Enterprise Mobility Suite (EMS) is a Cloud software management SaaS offering, which complements Office 365. EMS and similar SaaS tools are helpful in managing devices inside a business and providing a strong level of protection for users of Office 365. EMS manages the users' tools and the devices that they use (See Figure 4).

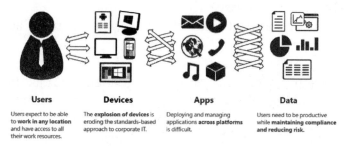

Users	Devices	Apps	Data
Users expect to be able to **work in any location** and have access to all their work resources.	The **explosion of devices** is eroding the standards-based approach to corporate IT.	Deploying and managing applications **across platforms** is difficult.	Users need to be productive while **maintaining compliance and reducing risk.**

Figure 4. Enterprise Mobility Suite – managing devices and data (courtesy of Microsoft)

Furthermore, tools like EMS are increasingly necessary as users are allowed to Bring Your Own Device (BYOD) to the workplace. As new users enter the workforce, they want to use their own devices, and load the software that they need to use to improve their personal productivity. This sounds like a win/win, and it can be so long as it does not come at the expense of network security. Through EMS and similar options, a business can remotely manage and remove company information from registered devices, as warranted necessary. The user end is addressed by Office 365, where they can use their own devices and they are managed by Windows Intune.

Back in the day, device management used to refer only to desktops. Today, we have multiple devices that fall into the category of "device management," including mobile devices, tablets, and laptops. Businesses need to manage all those devices, in addition to the device users, applications, and data. Office 365 and EMS fit this necessity because they are built with a self-service model which provides users access to Microsoft Cloud Services—worldwide. EMS provides consistent experiences for all users and the management of the devices. Users (and IT administrators) can add users to the local Active Directory, either through an Azure Join (Azure is the Microsoft Cloud that manages user security) or a traditional Active Directory Add User/Computer.

The Enterprise Mobility Suite provides consistency of device management with:
- Azure Join, which allows you to dynamically add a device with multi-factor authentication
- Domain-joined systems, which offers the ability to download and select Windows Intune
- Consistent opt-in message across all environments
- Consistent implementation of self-service portals across all environments

All the nuances of device management are important, and tools like Office 365 provide a self-service portal (e.g., it allows users to install licensed software on demand or reset their own password) that is extended with Windows Intune. This trend is forcing a change to the management of devices: application distribution via a company-owned application store. An IT manager will want to control the applications installed on all devices to reduce the security threat to your business. Microsoft EMS is one of the tools we use with SaaS Cloud services to accomplish this task.

As a business owner managing these activities (See Figure 5), you have a single view of all of the devices, including Apple and Android devices. Device management with integrated Office 365 support is made possible through the power of Windows Intune.

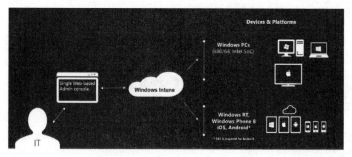

Figure 5. Enterprise Mobility Suite Management Console (courtesy of Microsoft)

CLOUD PROTECTION IS NOW A NECESSITY IN TODAY'S BUSINESS WORLD

When you look at all cloud applications, you need to consider the factors that we've discussed above. If you take any advice away from this, please take this: look at your business and understand what is important for the survival of it. The responsibility of doing so falls on the business owner, making it necessary o invest in the tools and security software that will ensure that business assets are secured.

About Matthew

Matt A. Katzer is the President of KAMIND IT, a Microsoft Gold Partner, and author of the best-selling book: *Under Attack.* He has also authored two cloud books: *Office 365: Managing and Migrating Your Business in the Cloud* and *Moving to Office 365: Planning and Migration Guide.* He is currently the President of the local chapter of IAMCP (International Association of Microsoft Channel Partners) and active in local business communities.

Matt's focus on cyber-security solutions started in the early 1990s while working in the security division of Intel Corporation. He holds a BSEE from the University of Michigan and an Executive MBA from the University of Oregon. Matt's greatest satisfaction comes from helping his customers become competitive in an increasingly technology-driven world.

CHAPTER 12

BEATING BAD GUYS AT THEIR OWN GAME

USING AUTOMATION FOR PREVENTION

BY HAL LONAS, CTO WEBROOT, INC.

The cybersecurity landscape has changed.

In this fast-paced world, cybercrime moves quickly and stealthily. The threats are more dangerous and coming at us faster than ever before. For most people, it's impossible to keep up, but for me and my team at Webroot, we are driven to not only keep up, but to move ahead.

Let's go back to the beginning. Initially, operating systems, the internet, databases, and networks were all designed by academics. This was great, of course, because they all worked together, trusted each other and created systems that were designed to help the world by allowing people to access ever more information. These academics were collegial and trusting, the only "bad guys" were amateurs, hobbyists, and those who were simply curious about computer technology. It worked great until real criminals found the flaws in the system.

The first cyber threats were comical and harmless. There may have been a little character that just started running across your computer screen. It was annoying and a bit distracting, but that was about it. Maybe the text you typed would start flashing a different color. Again, bothersome but not damaging. The first hackers wanted to show off and gain some notoriety. They were developing a persona and people talked about them in great detail. These guys made headline news to satisfy their egos. Then they were caught and soon forgotten. However, they inspired a new generation of hackers who craved more power and saw opportunity for financial gain from flaws in the internet and computers. It is those people that threaten us today.

THE MODERN LANDSCAPE

The dangers in the threat landscape escalate each passing day.

At first, advancements in cybercrime scared us, but didn't paralyze us. Flaws such as Y2K and date time bomb exploits were both imagined and real. Today, the game has escalated further and its rapid rise now includes significant global threats, which include:

- Economic shock and impact (stocks, trading, and corporate sabotage)
- Closing down public transportation and airports
- Military threats and release of top secret documents compromising national security
- Theft of intellectual property
- Theft of confidential consumer information

It's no longer just bothersome, it's costly and frightening. This modern landscape is far different to the old one.

*Today's cybercriminals are focused less on notoriety
and more on money.*

Criminals see opportunity to make financials gains through various methods:
- Selling private information on the internet black market—identity theft
- Crippling businesses through the use of encrypting ransomware— pay up or you don't get your data back
- Stealing national secrets for gain, economic advantage, or to promote a cause—think Julian Assange and WikiLeaks
- Making an enterprise of criminal activity by creating kits that help new criminals get into the cybercrime business—these kits are well developed exploit kits created by professionals with bad intent

- Dynamically generated phishing sites—these domains make it look like you're going to PayPal, eBay, or another reputable site, but you're really going to a fake that will steal your information (credit card numbers, passwords, etc.)
- Dark websites that are built to evade security software and circumvent the crawlers and scanners that catalogue the web—hidden on the long tail of the internet, where they don't register on searches immediately, but they do take advantage of search engine optimization (SEO) to lure in curious browsers and exploit the unwary

To criminals, the vastness of the internet is like the endless frontier—it will always be there and they are eager to venture further than anyone else and stake a claim for criminal activity. Then there are organizations like Webroot. **We are the ones who create the defenses that stop cybercriminals dead in their tracks by understanding them better and operating smarter.** It can be done. We've played an awful lot of catch-up, but now we're getting ready to pass them by.

THE OLD WAY OF DEFEATING THREATS

Manually intensive processes that are trying to compete against computerized technology rarely stand a chance.

Since security threats were so few and far between and "looked and felt" the same, we grew dependent on threat researchers. These researchers are smart people who understand what the criminals are up to and constantly gather data (as much as time will allow) to protect businesses and individuals. Antivirus companies and security officers at large corporations prided themselves on hiring these folks and advertised it. It showed they were committed to cybersecurity and safer than their competitors. Little did they realize that these displays were a challenge to cybercriminals.

Although threat researchers were successful at catching cybercriminals, it was infrequent enough that malware was actually named, just like hurricanes (iloveyou, CodeRed, Sasser, Zeus, etc.). Media would report the story, the bad guys would go away, and then their creations would be placed in the database of known threats. This was used for legacy antivirus and it worked because it could identify these known viruses by their signatures. The system sounds ideal at first glance, but what happened when the number of threats began to outnumber the number of researchers? Research fell behind!

THE CRIMINALS VERSUS THE COLLEGIATE

Criminals found ways to overwhelm the defenses by using the Internet to up their game.

Some time ago, I was invited to a paintball outing with some people that worked for the same company. I told them that I'd never played before, but they said that wasn't a problem. So okay, I was in.

Saturday came and off we went to paintball battle. The pros were dressed in the right gear, had automatic rapid fire "markers" (guns), and were completely prepared. Me—the newbie—had what the paintball place had to rent, and it showed my greenhorn status. So there I was with my pea shooter going up against the experts. I had a single shot and had to reload it every time I fired—if it fired at all. I was completely overwhelmed by the experience and seriousness of the pros. It did not go well and I was soon well "marked."

My point is: When you pit manually intensive efforts against automation, you are not armed to win this battle. Criminals are masterfully equipped, using what amounts to asymmetric warfare to wage an unfair fight. When threats are attacking a human from many directions, one is going to slip through the cracks while they are focused on another. Eventually, more get through the cracks than anyone realizes. This is the prelude to impending disaster if we don't start thinking like the criminals and using technology to compete at or above their level.

WE'RE TAKING ACTION

When criminals are the problem, beating them at their own game is a good remedy.

Webroot is devoted to fighting fire with fire and using technology to help give the good guys an edge. The criminals have had their way long enough. To do this, it all begins with using good machines to fight bad machines.

We have to think about our defenses differently in order to level the playing field. That means we have to adopt the same attitude and approach as the bad guys. We look at the picture as a whole from their perspective, and seek out the small loopholes that become doorways for criminals. Think of the approach a detective takes to catch a criminal—they dive into their strongest methodologies in order to solve the crime.

We now have the ability to teach machines what they need to know by giving them examples of what the bad guys do. Watson, the IBM computer, uses a similar approach to ours, but we are solving a different problem. Each piece of information that we feed this computer system makes it smarter; it grows more skilled to combat cybercrime. Here's how it works:

> We give the computer an example of a virus or malware. Let's say Cryptolocker (a popular malware virus). We watch it right at the infected machine so we can observe it operating in its native environment. Through this evaluation, the computer begins to understand it better, because it watches every bad behavior via a local threat lab. The details are monitored and the data is collected via cloud technology—not just human threat research. This leads to better understanding of the risk and how it works, exactly. Furthermore, by doing this, we can teach sensors, detectors, and machines what to watch for. Machines don't get tired and can keep watch 24 hours a day, 7 days a week.

The process of using the computer to evaluate the programs that are installed and their behaviors allows us to avoid using rigid rules and outdated methodologies. Being able to gain intelligence through evaluating behavioral patterns allows us to learn more about cyber activity and patterns in today's world. Through behavioral assessment we can identify common cybercrime patterns such as:

- A new program on my computer is capturing my credit card number.
- My computer files are being encrypted by someone, and it isn't me.
- My private data is being sent directly to the cloud without my permission.

These patterns are all indicative of unsolicited cybercriminal activity and they are just three examples of hundreds.

By using modern technologies and tools such as big data to search for bad actors and patterns, we are making progress. The cloud is a great resource for us, because it connects users and observations, which makes the computer smarter with each bit of information it receives—and it's constantly receiving new information. This concept can best be compared to the medical concept of inoculating the herd. That is how diseases such as Small Pox or Polio have been practically eradicated. When using this concept in reference to computer security, everyone participates in the neighborhood watch program and the bad guys end up with nowhere to go. Eventually, they give up and shut down.

Shutting down a criminal sounds great, right? Of course some get away, and they go back to work on their next attempt at crime. If they use similar methodologies, that makes it easy to find them, but even new bad behaviors are quickly discovered and shut down. It's through having machines that do this constantly and tirelessly, that we are gaining ground on criminals and overtaking them with "anticipate, protect, and defend" technology. And better yet, every attempt they make creates a smarter machine working against them.

A MORE SECURE FUTURE

The only way to get ahead and stay ahead is with automation.

It's essential to have a system in place that can update threats as we find them. Threats do not take a vacation, which means the method which we choose to fight them cannot either. Webroot is truly relentless in our pursuit to protect everyone, anywhere. We know that no matter how much security you have in place, if you let down your defenses for an instant, you could be in trouble. Suddenly your rock-solid defensive wall becomes as porous as a sponge, rendering it ineffective.

By having a super computer whose only purpose is to better understand all cyber threats so it can shut them down, the good guys will exhaust the bad guys. This won't come without absolute commitment, however, since the criminals remain highly motivated for profit.

By reducing manmade security and incorporating technologically advanced, smart technology we can make this vision a reality. It's happening now and the tide is changing, making a world where we can all feel safer using the technology that has become a part of our lives and will not be going away. Being human is wonderful, but expecting only humans to protect us in the limitless virtual world is an impossible request.

Using automation for prevention is the only answer.

About Hal

Hal Lonas is the Chief Technology Officer at Webroot, a privately held Internet security firm that provides state-of-the-art, cloud-based endpoint security and threat intelligence software and service solutions. Mr. Lonas has a special interest in machine learning and automation as applied to security problems as legacy systems become overrun by new threats.

Previously the Senior VP of Product Engineering for Webroot, Mr. Lonas has more than 25 years of engineering development and management experience in software ventures from startups to Fortune 500 firms. He joined Webroot via the acquisition of BrightCloud, where he was a founder and VP Engineering. In the past Mr. Lonas has held key engineering management positions with Websense (WBSN), ADP and others, and has co-authored numerous patents. He holds a Bachelor of Science degree in Aeronautics and Astronautics from MIT.

CHAPTER 13

BUSINESS REALITIES OF COMPLIANCE PENALTIES FROM DATA BREACH

BY KEVIN FREAM

It takes 20 years to build a reputation and five minutes to ruin it. If you think about that, you'll do things differently.
~ Warren Buffet

In the 2011 movie "Moneyball", General Manager Billy Beane provides an insightful lesson showing how to release players in a succinct straightforward manner. Just like that illustrative scene, you need to know there is no silver bullet answer for preventing data breach – much less avoiding the corresponding compliance penalties affecting virtually every business. Unlike releasing a player as in the movie, publicized data breaches are guaranteed to have severe backlash including damaged reputation.

Business owners and management teams should literally take a lesson from the approach and title of the book Moneyball: The Art of Winning an Unfair Game. Whether you lean politically toward the left or right, no one can deny that government compliance programs and taxes continue to rise. In spite of the U.S. Small Business Administration 2006 re-launch of Business.USA.Gov, small and medium-sized businesses are especially easy targets and largely unaware of compliance penalties.

Aristotle put forth the concept that ignorance of the law is no excuse in approximately 340 B.C. His words still ring true today, as common unawareness does not remove your liability for violating the law.

Compliance penalties can be shockingly devastating by delivering hefty fines and potential prison time, instead of the misguided myth of simply paying a nominal fine when you get caught.

You can blindly copy your competition by taking a cost-of-doing-business approach toward government compliance, or leverage smart ideas and build a better product/service for customers. Savvy organizations will primarily focus upon a vector approach to reducing complexity and avoiding risk, as well as the true costs of compliance violations explained in the following sections.

VECTOR GROWTH APPROACH TO TECHNOLOGY

In 1973, the Harvard Business Review published an evolution of Information Technology (IT) presented by Richard Nolan as the stages of a technology growth model. Although enhanced from four to six stages a decade later, the Nolan Growth Model is a dated premise based upon the fallacy of economic growth rather than practical business need.

Generally, all organizations today utilize and can afford necessary technology. It's extremely rare that IT Managers have any significant budget authority. Further, startup companies regularly disrupt all industries, dispelling a widely-perpetuated marketing pitch that the more you spend on technology, the more competitive your company.

Ask yourself who benefits from an IT department focused solely on growing its own fiefdom? Who gains from having a costly patchwork of layers of hardware and software from various vendors for significant complexity? The answer is definitely not owners, shareholders, or customers – which is why discerning leaders and management teams implement the Vector Model as shown below.

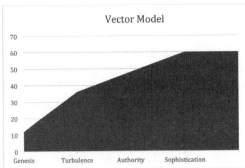

Source: streamliningtechnology.com

Genesis is the beginning stage in implementing technology solutions based upon reduced complexity, rather than by the budget of technical features. The concept starts with an initial understanding that some services are recommended to be outsourced at a far less cost with greater productivity and security than any do-it-yourself approaches, which may misleadingly seem more cost effective.

Turbulence is the following step wherein management begins to take a lead role in fully understanding technology strategy and implementation, as opposed to abdicating leadership to the accounting or technology personnel within a company. The result is old paradigms of support and purchasing are both challenged and streamlined.

70% of companies fail to transition from Turbulence to Authority.

Next is Authority, in which critical services are consolidated and therefore the risk is distributed across a smaller number of products and services. The organization then begins publishing intellectual property as a differentiator in being both more trustworthy than their competitors and offering more value for customers.

The last phase is called Sophistication which entails the organization evaluating their return on investment, while continuing to focus on better customer experience. Special emphasis by management is taken in reviewing processes for any business improvement with the consideration of new technology.

Once you identify the current operational stage of technology within your organization, you have a better understanding of weaknesses. Therefore, you can begin to evaluate a breakeven between technology costs and business improvement versus the risk of compliance penalties. Unfortunately, an estimated seventy percent of businesses are so resistant to change that they never make it past the Turbulence stage. As evidenced by research every few years by Forbes and Bloomberg, this obstinate lot eventually fails in their endeavors. Industry forces like unexpected compliance penalties just hasten their demise.

STATURE DAMAGE MODEL: REAL COST OF COMPLIANCE VIOLATIONS

In most businesses employees and owners think of compliance penalties like a traffic fine. You had the bad luck to get caught and you pay the fee and move on. However, unlike a mere traffic ticket, the highest cost of compliance penalties from data breach is actually your damaged reputation. The reason why is twofold: you are legally required to publicize a breach for the protection of current and future customers, and then there is the overstated, yet true notion, that nothing on the Internet ever really goes away.

Until relatively recently, many organizations could simply shun or ignore compliance risk without the Internet as a factor. What's the cost of doing nothing? Who's going to know? Well, the cost of doing nothing is often zero, but only until some catastrophic event like exorbitant compliance penalties and related lost revenue materialize. While Fox Business reported in 2014 that the odds of the IRS auditing a business with $1 million or more in sales is just 12.1%, the odds of a data breach penalty are nearly 25%.

The Office of Civil Rights (Division of U.S. Department of Health and Human Services) actively audits health-related organizations for privacy violations. Also, banks and related financial institutions review merchant data security standards annually to protect cardholder payment information. Finally, the Federal Trade Commission is scheduled to aggressively investigate all types of businesses for proper disposal of customer and employee information because of widespread identify theft.

Not only are government agencies reviewing compliance, but practically anyone can be a whistle-blower for privacy and data breach concerns. Employee, vendors, customers, and competitors can all report compliance violations and trigger audits and penalties as stated in the publically viewable sites below:

HIPAA: http://www.hhs.gov/hipaa/filing-a-complaint
PCI-DSS: https://www.mastercard.us/en-us/consumers/
           get-support/report-problem-shopping.html
FACTA: https://www.ftccomplaintassistant.gov/

The true cost of compliance violations is worsened by lost revenue and productivity, purchase of additional security products and services, lost future income due to negative publicity, and then penalties with on-going audit often required afterward.

Reputation Damage Calculator		
Top Concerns: security breach reasons, penalties, security costs, and future prevention.		
Scenarios	**Value**	**Units**
Outage Duration	8	Hours
Employeess Affected	12	Employees
Productivity Loss	100%	Percentage
Revenue non-recoverable	100%	Percentage
Average Employee Cost	$22	Hourly
Average Employee Reveneue	$104	Hourly
Intagible Cost	$11	Hourly
Productivity Loss	$3,168	Violation
Revenue Loss	$9,984	Violation
Intangible Loss	$0	Violation
Compliance Penalties	$10,000	Incident
Added Security Products/Services	$12,000	Incident
Total Loss	**$35,152**	

Source: cyberprey.com

The worst part is not only regulatory authorities publicizing penalty violations and your own data breach notice, but the realization that such negative publicity is saved with easy access at archive.org. Years after a publicized data breach notice is removed from any web site, prospective customers or cunning competitors may search for old breach pages. Using common search tools like Ahrefs.com, anyone can view broken links to an old non-existent web page and copy the exact address to search on "Wayback Machine" (https://archive.org/web/).

Medical and health data breaches are regularly listed at: www.cdph. ca.gov/programs/Pages/LnCBreachConfidential.aspx. Large business data breaches are also listed at sec.gov.

TOP THREE COMPLIANCE PENALTY CONCERNS

The amount of potential taxes and other compliance liabilities for business owners seems to grow each year, as evidenced with new legislation like the Affordable Care Act. Large publicly-traded organizations also have their own unique set of compliance challenges with Sarbanes Oxley. For most other businesses, there are three major compliance concerns all generally focused on privacy issues: Health Insurance Portability and Accounting Act (HIPAA), Payment Card Industry Data Security Standard (PCI-DSS), and Fair and Accurate Credit Transactions Act (FACTA).

President Bill Clinton signed the infamous HIPAA into law in 1996. The portion that affects all employers (not just medical and insurance entities) is the policies, procedures, and guidelines for maintaining the privacy and security of individually identifiable health information. Unauthorized disclosure (printed or digital documents) of individually identifiable health information may be reported to the Office of Civil Rights for investigation and penalty assessment.

HIPAA Violation	Minimum Penalty	Maximum Penalty
Individual did not know (and by exercising reasonable diligence would not have known) that he/she violated HIPAA	$100 per violation, with an annual maximum of $25,000 for repeat violations (Note: maximum that can be imposed by State Attorneys General regardless of the type of violation)	$50,000 per violation, with an annual maximum of $1.5 million
HIPAA violation due to reasonable cause and not due to willful neglect	$1,000 per violation, with an annual maximum of $100,000 for repeat violations	$50,000 per violation, with an annual maximum of $1.5 million
HIPAA violation due to willful neglect but violation is corrected within the required time period	$10,000 per violation, with an annual maximum of $250,000 for repeat violations	$50,000 per violation, with an annual maximum of $1.5 million
HIPAA violation is due to willful neglect and is not corrected	$50,000 per violation, with an annual maximum of $1.5 million	$50,000 per violation, with an annual maximum of $1.5 million

The "Payment Card Industry Security Standards Council" was formed on December 15, 2004 for policies between the major credit card brands of Visa, MasterCard, American Express, Discover, and JCB. PCI-DSS is a proprietary information security standard aimed at reducing fraud and identity theft for the many organizations that handle major credit cards. Violations primarily involve data breach by hackers due to inadequate security processes and systems or disclosing more than the last four digits of a card in digital or printed form.

PCI Penalties
Fines up to $500,000 per data security incident
Fines up to $50,000 per day for non-compliance with published standards
Liability for all fraud losses incurred from compromised account numbers
Liability for the cost of re-issuing cards associated with the compromise
Suspension of merchant accounts

President George W. Bush signed FACTA into law in 2003. Most people understand that FACTA allows individuals access to a free credit report annually, but what is not commonly known is that it requires secure disposal of employee and customer information for businesses. The Federal Trade Commission announced that in 2016 it will begin randomly auditing organizations of all sizes due to the rampant problem of identity theft. Common violations for FACTA are failure to shred or delete employee or customer documents or inadequate digital security: https://www.ftc.gov/tips-advice/business-center/guidance/disposing-consumer-report-information-rule-tells-how

FACTA
Federal Trade Commission has not published a defined schedule to date, but will likely pattern after HIPAA penalties. Fines up to $500,000 per data security incident
Violators may also face state fines and possible civil action.

Organizations are required to publicly publish anything that constitutes as major violations and contact customers in writing concerning breach or potential breach of private information, potentially ruining a company's reputation. A poor but common practice is a single form or database which includes complete employee information including medical claims. Any business or organization that follows this practices and takes credit card payments, may then be in violation and penalized for all three compliance areas above.

REGULAR EXAMINATION OF RISK AND IMPROVEMENT

While your competition takes an apathetic or cost-of-doing-business approach, the best advice to avoid compliance penalties is taking a business improvement approach. A regular Cyber Security Exam is cheap insurance and any improvement in business process or security is a differentiator to publicize to customers.

A Cyber Security Exam is the purview of qualified IT security firms and not accountants or lawyers. Legitimate firms follow the Vector Model to try and eliminate complexity and costs. Exams should be performed by degreed and certified professionals with more than 10 years' experience in technology security. Most exams will cost between $3,000 and $7,000 depending upon the size and complexity of the customer organization and may include an Acceptable Use Policy (AUP). Qualified firms may also act as a defense for government compliance audit like a CPA or an attorney representing a client. In the process, your existing IT staff gains some accountability while you gain peace of mind.

Good marketing builds trust with a preponderance of evidence for prospective customers. Press releases, blog posts, videos, and compliance logos are all important to provide a positive impression and your continual commitment to improvement for existing customers. In all businesses there is a human element. If you do suffer a breach and compliance penalty, you have a basis to evaluate failures from the last exam and more importantly, you have many positive listings to push anything negative down in Google search results.

About Kevin

As the CEO of Matrixforce Corporation, Kevin Fream brings twenty-five years of experience as a cyber-security advisor to prospective customers. He specializes in helping business owners and leadership teams reduce technological complexity and avoid risk, with an emphasis on highlighting current compliance penalties that impact the viability of nearly every business.

While Kevin was completing his Bachelor of Science in Management Information Systems degree from the University of Tulsa, he landed a paid internship with DuPont. That early experience with one of the most security conscious organizations in the nation allowed him to go on to work nationwide with a number of other Fortune 500 firms.

Along the way, he noted that the local marketplace was riddled with suspect competencies, rude behavior, and relentless hourly billing. Mid-sized businesses of $5 million to $150 million in revenue seem to be particularly under-served and mistreated. As a result, Kevin formulated a distinct customer service strategy:

1) Assume the risk for customers by offering flat cost and demonstrating business justification. No one would be compensated for billable hours or selling products.
2) Train staff on rules of engagement and how to talk with customers in simple language, so that they can understand and control outcomes for Information Technology.
3) Specialize in Microsoft productivity and security solutions for annually-audited expertise.

Today, Matrixforce has saved clients collectively over $500 million on technology services and products and is a top 100 Microsoft Gold Cloud Partner.

More cyber-security insights, tools, and downloads may be accessed at Cyberprey. com. Look for Kevin's next book being published soon: *Revealing Secrets to Streamlining Technology.*

Contact information:
- kfream@matrixforce.com
- http://www.linkedin.com/in/kevinfream

CHAPTER 14

UNBREAKABLE
– PASSWORD SECURITY FOR YOUR BUSINESS

BY MILTON BARTLEY

If you are reading this, the chances are you have one or more work and online accounts in which passwords are mandatory. A recent study revealed that the average person now has nineteen passwords to remember. (I personally have over two-hundred passwords in my password program.) Given that, it is no wonder people are tempted to reuse the same password for multiple accounts. Passwords are the most common security measure that companies and programs offer and they are used to identify individuals and secure their identities and data. They have become as ubiquitous as the services and devices on which they are used, from computers, to smartphones, to bank accounts, to video games, to social media. Despite years of technological advancement, users [read: employees] are still the weakest link in the security chain. No matter how effective a security policy you create, user error can render the security useless. And studies show that the most common way user accounts are compromised is through breached email. Consider, then, how vital a strong password policy is to a small business.

I recently received an urgent call from a client in the mortgage industry telling me about a possible email hack at their company. The day before, one of their closing attorneys received an email [ostensibly] from a client for whom he was performing a mortgage closing. The email - from the client's correct email address and addressed correctly to the closing attorney - asked simply that, when the funding was processed, he wire the funds to their bank. The email included all the proper routing instructions and account information instructions for their new bank. You can guess what happened next. That's right, he wired over $300,000 to the wrong place.

Didn't they have a procedure to verify the bank account information received by email? Yes, they did, but the attorney did not follow protocol (that's a different chapter), and the money was lost. Unfortunately, this is all too common of a tale.

So how does this tie into password security? The company's email was not, in fact, compromised. The client's was, however, and that is the crux of this chapter. People who have the correct password security protocols in place at work all too often ignore those best practices with personal accounts, especially personal email accounts.

As I just mentioned, the client's email account had been hacked. We have all been the recipient of a spam message from a "friend's" account...the telltale sign that their email has been hacked. Frighteningly, however, the more sophisticated hackers don't send spam email or leave any clues that they are reading your email. They watch, read, and wait for their opportunity. That is exactly what happened here.

When a sophisticated hacker gets into your email, they can gain insight into every facet of your life. For most of us, someone spending a week reading through our email history will learn our banking, investing, childcare, business, and shopping habits, not to mention the personal messages between friends and family members. If this gives you the creeps, GOOD; it should.

A BRIEF HISTORY OF PASSWORDS

Passwords have been used for centuries, dating back to the early origins of the Roman Empire when the Roman military used watchwords to identify their sentries. Societies evolved that usage over time. However, in this chapter we will be focusing exclusively on digital passwords. While historians can't pinpoint exactly when passwords were first introduced into computing, they do largely agree that the first computer password was created at the Massachusetts Institute of Technology (MIT) in conjunction with their Compatible Time-Sharing System (CTSS) in the early 1960s.

In 1962, computers were largely mysteries to the general public, but not to Dr. Allen Scherr, an MIT research fellow. Frustrated by the system limits on his allotted computing time, he found a way to print out all the passwords in the system. He then used other users' passwords to gain additional computing time. He shared the list with several colleagues so they could do the same. This was the very first password breach on record.

Prior to 1980, computers were primarily confined to big business and government usage. In the mid-1970s, however, when it became evident that personal computers were more than a fad, the government and the computing industry adopted a program aimed to encrypt and thus secure passwords and other digital information, titled Data Encryption Standard (DES). This encryption protocol remained the gold standard for twenty years.

In 1997, a group of ethical hackers cracked the encryption in DES and showed that computing power had evolved to the point that cracking the encryption was no longer theoretical. Shortly thereafter, the Advanced Encryption Standard (AES) was adopted as the new standard. AES is still the primary encryption standard in use today and is the only publicly accessible cipher approved by the National Security Agency (NSA) for top secret information.

RISKS OF PASSWORD EXPOSURE

For many companies and individuals, our most critical business and personal data is kept digitally and is guarded by passwords. A password breach can expose information that could be used for identity theft, financial fraud, blackmail, or other illicit activities. The Identity Theft Resource Center (ITRC), a national resource on consumer issues related to cybersecurity, data breaches, social media, fraud, scams and other issues tracks all incidents in which an individual is potentially put at risk because of exposure. The ITRC breaks data loss into seven categories: insider theft, hacking, data on the move, subcontractor/third-party, employee error/negligence, accidental web/internet exposure, and physical theft. In 2015, the ITRC reported that hacking represented 37.9 percent breach incidents, followed by the employee error/negligence at 14.9 percent. Thus, more than 50% of reported breaches in 2015 were directly or indirectly related to lax password security.

The most serious issues with password breaches occur when financial or self-identifying information such as social security numbers or PIN numbers are compromised. The exposure or loss of your personal information can be devastating and can have lasting repercussions. If your business is responsible for the exposure of hundreds, thousands, or even millions of records, however, the financial and reputational damage can be catastrophic. A recent study commissioned by Scott & Scott, LLP, a law and technology services firm focusing on data privacy and network security, found that after a reported data breach, 74% reported a loss of customers, 59% faced potential litigation, 33% faced potential fines, and 32% experienced a decline in share value. In addition, one of the largest reported reasons for reported breaches was negligent employees, temporary employees, and/or contractors. Again, bad password security was a primary driver of data breaches.

Interestingly, many of these same organizations were also found to have lax or outdated password security protocols. In fact, many of the organizations responsible for reported breaches had no documented password policy. Creating a strong password policy is a critical step to ensure that employees safeguard the systems they rely on every day. A complex password protocol can seem like an inconvenience to many users, but that must not prevent you from creating, implementing and maintaining a strong password policy in your organization.

Remember, the easiest way for a hacker or bad-actor to gain access to your network is through user negligence. Examples of this negligence include: using the same password for business and personal accounts, keeping passwords in a document on their computer, keeping password(s) written down on or in their desk, accessing company resources (email, software, etc.) using a public computer or public Wi-Fi, and sharing passwords with other employees.

SHARED PASSWORDS

Do you or somebody that you know share a Netflix, Hulu, or Amazon account with somebody outside of your household? This is a prime example of password sharing, and although shared online movie and television show programs are typically not a threat in and of themselves, sharing passwords in other areas can be devastating. Simply put, the practice of sharing passwords among two or more employees is unacceptable. Once more than one person knows a password, it becomes virtually impossible to determine who performed a task and when that task was performed. The nightmare scenario is the rogue employee who abuses system access privileges. It doesn't happen often, but when it does, the results can be fairly devastating. Not every insider hack or data theft is the result of using a shared password, but a shared password – particularly a shared administrative password – is a weakness that no business should tolerate.

PROCESSES AND PROCEDURES

As a small business owner, password security is – or at least should be – a central part of your overall security protocol. Any policy you create or amend should help to defeat guessing/dictionary attacks, raw brute-force attacks, and attacks against common password patterns (like Qwerty123!). Most software systems today help you create and enforce strong password policies. Strong policy characteristics include password length, mix of alphanumeric characters and symbols, and enforced password history – as well as a minimum "age" requirement (to prevent employees from simply changing their password as many times in a row as necessary to reuse their original password).

The trap I see business owners fall into all too often, however, is simply not using the tools at their disposal. Specifically, they fail to enforce these simple requirements on all company systems, but most often on email accounts. As cognizant as business owners are about IT security and the need for strong policies and procedures, I continue to be surprised at the number of business owners I counsel who place convenience ahead of security, particularly with regards to email passwords. Because email has become such an integral part of our work and personal lives, and because we can access it across so many of our devices, changing that password and updating it across all those devices can be cumbersome.

Thus, business owners ignore the best advice available to them, often to their detriment.

So how do you enforce a password policy that embodies all these complex choices while knowing that we must have so many passwords to remember, and must keep them straight, even though we cannot write them down or type them into a "secure" document? The choices are limited, and until biometric technology catches up – or on – the options are multi-factor and/or a password storage program/app.

Biometric security has been around for years, but it took Apple and the iPhone fingerprint reader to take it mainstream. Apple has sold more than 480 million iPhones with fingerprint technology (worldwide). Many of us are now perfectly comfortable trusting our fingerprint to unlock our smartphone – arguably the bank vault of our digital lives. But how does that translate to the workplace? How soon will fingerprint readers, facial recognition and voice print become mainstream? Experts differ in their opinions, and regardless, not today, right?

So how can you and your employees safely access critical systems that are and must be, password protected, AND keep password protocols in place, AND keep employees from going rogue to avoid having to remember dozens of passwords? Let's examine these options.

Multi-factor authentication is one of the most cost-effective mechanisms businesses can use to protect digital assets. As more businesses move their precious data and their servers into the cloud, better authentication has moved from a "should probably do" to an "absolutely must implement" status. In simple terms, multi-factor, or two-factor authentication adds a second security criterion to your login process. In addition to the standard username and password, users must authenticate with a "second factor." Examples range from the simple, like verifying a previously selected picture or a piece of personal data, or connecting to a virtual private network (VPN) prior to logging into protected resources; to the intermediate like a one-time password or pin – OTP – that is sent to the user's mobile phone via text or SMS; to the complex, like using a token, app, or card with a rolling PIN that changes at periodic intervals. Multi-factor systems are standard protocol in enterprise organizations, and competition in the market has reduced both price and complexity to the levels that small and medium-sized businesses can invest in and easily implement effective systems.

Password managers have become more and more common as well. Password managers store your login information for all the applications and websites you use and help you both create and securely store multiple passwords; most can help you log into the applications and websites automatically. Password managers encrypt your password database with a master password, and that master password is the only one you have to remember. Businesses can take advantage of this service with software that includes sharing and management of individual and system passwords from a centrally administered platform. The best of these platforms offer cross-platform interoperability (Mac, Windows and Mobile), offer multi-factor options, incorporate biometrics in the iPhone and iOS, and will run periodic password audits that help find weak and duplicate passwords and rank users' password postures.

CONCLUSION

It is not the author's intention to scare you, but rather to heighten your awareness. After reading this you may conclude that, as great as it sounds to have strong password policies in place, it is simply too much of a burden to place on your employees and yourself. I hope this is not the case, however, and that you recognize how important password security is to the long-term success of your organization.

About Milton

Milton Bartley is one of Nashville's most recognizable business leaders. From serving as a combat leader in the United States Army to launching a world-class IT services company, his drive to achieve has led him to the fulfillment of a better life for himself, his family and his employees.

In 2007, Milton co-founded ImageQuest, and it quickly became one of Nashville's fastest growing technology companies. ImageQuest is recognized as a pioneer in IT services, IT security, and business communications, specializing in outsourced IT for service-oriented businesses that have a compliance or regulatory oversight component to their business.

Milton is passionate about serving the community both personally and through his business. Milton and ImageQuest are committed to addressing some of the community's most complex problems through technological innovation and support. One of Milton's personal passions is High Hopes Development Center in Franklin, Tennessee. High Hopes is a 501(c)(3) nonprofit organization whose mission is to equip children and youth with the skills necessary to achieve success through education, rehabilitation, and loving support. Milton serves on the Board of Directors at High Hopes.

Milton holds a bachelor's degree from Virginia Tech and a Master's in Business Administration from Xavier University. For the past two years, Milton has been included in the MSPMentor Top 250, recognizing the world's top managed services provider (MSP) executives, entrepreneurs and experts. Milton believes "It takes a team of committed individuals to build and grow a business in today's world of rapidly changing technology."

You can connect with Milton at:
- mbartley@myimagequest.com
- www.linkedin.com/in/miltonbartley
- www.myimagequest.com/milton-bartley/

CHAPTER 15

PCI, HIPAA, AND SOX
– GOVERNMENT REGULATORY COMPLIANCE

BY NICK ESPINOSA

Welcome to the most exciting chapter in this book! Who doesn't love to discuss government regulatory compliance? As a security fanatic who lives and breathes these standards, I actually enjoy planning, testing, and executing security solutions for PCI, HIPAA, and SOX compliance. Then, I try to break the solutions. It's real fun for a security nerd!

Recently, one of my clients was part of the pilot program to introduce medical marijuana dispensaries across our state. These facilities are under intense scrutiny. The state is looking for anything to allow them to shutter the dispensaries and the media is eager to report anything on this newly formed industry. The need for strict adherence to HIPAA standards and security is intense and must be thoroughly verified, creating a lot of stress for the owners of these facilities. Owners must rely on their IT support to properly configure and protect their network. Otherwise, they possibly face large fines or even being shut down if the violation is severe enough.

After walking my client through the IT plan to setup and secure their data network, we worked with the contractor who was going to install their alarm system and corresponding multitude of video cameras. We completed the installation and configured the network to adhere to HIPAA and state compliances. After the install, we ran our standard penetration testing to ensure our configuration was correct and protected from the outside world.

We found an issue, a major one. The company who installed the alarm system and video cameras installed a security controller onto the network running an old operating system, one easily breached. Essentially, because this contractor required us to expose the security controller to the Internet, my HIPAA compliant client was now exposed to attack and their video cameras could have been remotely controlled by hackers or their alarm system disabled remotely. Had we not adhered to best practices for HIPAA, this client could have been compromised and we, as the IT security consultants, would have been liable for damages under the law. This experience proves a well-thought out plan, along with execution and testing, is critical to ensure compliance is properly implemented.

Along with HIPAA, PCI and SOX are two other major laws which set standards for government compliance. Each has common themes in terms of security configuration and standards but also very notable differences. All three require planning and implementing a specific IT infrastructure in order to be compliant. There are many other government compliances out there; SEC for financial traders, ITAR for arms trafficking control and on and on. These three compliances, HIPAA, PCI, and SOX, were chosen because they're broad in scope and also have planning phases that are rather similar to most government compliance standards out there.

To begin with, HIPAA, the "Health Insurance Portability and Accountability Act," is the governing standard for all medical facilities dealing with patient information. HIPAA was enacted in 1996 and is an umbrella law covering patients' rights. It was designed to fight discrimination based on health status and to ensure sensitive medical data is protected and under the patient's control. Traditionally, the government only investigated HIPAA violations when reported to HIPAA's governing body. That recently has changed. Thanks to the HITECH Act of 2009, there is a new standard for electronic medical records, their storage, and how to protect them. No longer will HIPAA wait for violators to be reported. There is now an army of HIPAA auditors proactively checking on medical practices to ensure proper adherence to the law. As of 2015, medical practices face severe penalties or loss of license for violations.

PCI is the largest in terms of the number of companies falling under the standard. PCI, formally known as PCI DSS, stands for "Payment Card Industry Data Security Standard." Launched in 2004, PCI's primary goal is to create a compliance standard to ensure any company accepting credit cards is properly securing the data collected on customers. Any merchant accepting credit cards is required by law to adhere to PCI compliance and is susceptible to audits by the PCI governing body. Penalties can include steep fines and even a revocation of the privilege to accept credit cards. PCI is an evolving standard, with new versions of security software, solutions, and appliances constantly emerging to combat the versatility of hackers. Therefore, constant testing and verification of PCI security standards is vital.

SOX is the smallest of the three compliances, in terms of population of companies required to adhere to the compliance. It also happens to be the most comprehensive and aggressive standard of the three. A former client once told me going through a SOX audit is "the equivalent of having a root canal while being examined by your proctologist."

SOX is the "Sarbanes-Oxley Act" enacted in 2002 in the wake of the Enron and WorldCom scandals. Primarily, it is directed at publicly-held corporations, though some private corporation provisions are there as well. Both types of corporations are required to create internal standards and procedures for handling and reporting financial information. From an IT perspective, this requires the entire network to be configured in a way that demonstrates compliance to every aspect of SOX. Failure to do so, or failing to have the redundancies needed to ensure mitigation in failure of data retention, will result in millions of dollars of fines and a possible shuttering of the corporation.

Before we dive into how to secure a network or infrastructure, it is important to understand the approach each governing body takes in terms of testing their respective compliance. Though they often look for similar items and configurations, the goal and focus of each is different.

PCI cares less about how the entire network is configured. Instead, it focuses on specific entities which fall under their jurisdiction; the protection of credit card user information. They want to ensure the database storing the information is properly secured from illegal access by users on the network, as well as hackers. Further, they must ensure any public facing entities which accept credit cards are secured and running the latest versions of software and security certificates. The basic testing for PCI compliance includes penetration testing of all public facing entities to ensure the surface area for attack is minimal. SSL/TLS certificates are checked, ecommerce software is checked to ensure there are no known vulnerabilities, and in-transit encryption is verified. A comprehensive PCI test will also include verification of at-rest encryption of the credit card processing database to ensure it cannot be illegally duplicated, as well as looking into the security policy, planning, and management of the systems.

HIPAA focuses on the avenues of user access at a medical practice to patient records and includes things like checking to make sure all users have a unique username and password for auditing purposes and remote access to HIPAA compliant data, how patient records are moved from location to location (physically and virtually), penetration and vulnerability testing, backup encryption verification, and more. Basically, any way a human could accidentally or intentionally disclose protected patient data is investigated. Even conversations between practitioners regarding patients is regulated, as well as how computer monitors are oriented in regards to eavesdropping by non-authorized individuals, such as other patients, within the facility. With new facilities, HIPAA auditing will include all of the above as well as inspections for privacy partitions, how rooms with compliant information are protected from non-authorized personnel, vulnerabilities in the data network, such as weak wireless security or guest access that is not properly isolated from the private network.

SOX is all about the paper trail and history. Because a company is required to create a process for control and data retention, a SOX audit is extremely comprehensive and will focus on how data is being entered, stored, and retained. A SOX audit is like an IRS audit on steroids! An external SOX auditor, not to be confused with a company's internal staff auditor (or paid contractor in some cases), seeks to verify all data, as it relates to the finances of a corporation, is readily available and verifiable as untampered with from the time of input. Gaps in the data are cause for serious concern and serve as red flags for a SOX audit, so ensuring retention is thorough and highly redundant is a must. Data, or business records, has a very broad definition within SOX and includes not only financial accounting records but any paperwork pertaining to finance, including email, recorded conversations, and directives to change financial information. SOX also requires the longest length of history in data retention. Similar to SEC compliance, SOX requires all data be archived and retained for no less than seven years. Some records, such as bank statements, charts of accounts, contracts, employee payroll records, legal correspondence, training manuals, and even union agreements must be kept permanently.

Now that you have a thorough overview of PCI, HIPAA and SOX it is time to take action! While it may seem overwhelming, following these eight steps across your network and systems can ensure compliance to PCI, HIPAA, and/or SOX:

1. **Create a baseline of understanding of your network status prior to ensuring compliance.** There are several testing tools available which allow you to run a basic compliance audit to determine vulnerabilities. These tools go a long way to helping understand just how much, or little, work is needed to bring the network up to code.

2. **Have an excellent backup schema, which includes back up and archive of data onsite and offsite, and conduct periodic restore tests.** Onsite will ensure quick and easy access to backups and offer the best performance when recovery is needed. Offsite provides disaster recovery in case of catastrophic failure of the infrastructure or destruction of the business site (fire, tornado, flood, etc.). Data loss can be tantamount to malfeasance in the eyes of a government audit, so this step is critical to achieving compliance.

3. **Encrypt data, and the platforms it resides on, to protect against loss, theft or malfeasance.** A theft or loss of more than fifty HIPAA compliant records constitutes a breach that must be reported to HIPAA, as well as local media and all patients within the practice. Theft of PCI compliant data can result in the loss of ability to accept credit cards. Loss of data in SOX is a violation of the data retention policy and can cost the company the right to conduct business. In each case, it's possible the business could be liable for millions of dollars in fines and damages, not to mention the loss of reputation.

4. **Ensure passwords are unique and complex enough to withstand attack, for all network appliances and servers.** Make sure all users on the network, from the janitors to the CEO, have a unique login and are set to be fully audited for any actions performed on the network.

5. **Enable Two Factor Authentication (2FA) whenever it is available with no exceptions.** This helps to ensure that no one can spoof a user both inside and outside of the network. 2FA uses a security device or cell phone to send a unique code that must be typed in when the user logs in. Don't have the device or phone in your possession and you cannot login.

6. **Maintain a security posture that minimizes the surface area for attack by a hacker.** This means closing ports in a firewall that don't need to be opened, not allowing remote access to network appliance consoles, accessing all data through an IPSec VPN when remote, isolating the public facing servers from the private ones, and creating a Unified Threat Management (UTM) profile for the network so threats and attacks can be analyzed quickly and dealt with in real time.

7. **Retain the services of a skilled consultant who is well-versed in the compliance standard your corporation requires.** Not all IT consultants are the same, nor do they all have the same breadth of knowledge. Hiring a consultant without a background in compliance means critical pieces of the compliance puzzle could be missed. A good consultant will be well-versed in the regulations that pertain to your business, will be able to develop a complete plan for IT compliance, and make choices throughout their tenure to keep the focus on properly maintaining these compliances.

8. **Periodically test adherence to compliances and standards to ensure nothing has changed or been missed.** The government loves to add addendums and make changes to the compliances. This can add an ever-increasing level of complexity to an existing network as a once compliant network can change to non-compliant within a short period of time.

While the aforementioned steps apply to all three compliance standards, each compliance standard has specific components requiring specific attention. The following details actions to take in order to comply to PCI, HIPAA, or SOX individually though all these points are good advice for everything.

I. PCI

1. Conduct penetration testing of the public-facing web server to identify and close any open firewall ports and holes.
2. Ensure SSL/TLS certificates are up to date and running the latest versions. There is no excuse for running an outdated certificate or one which is only secured using SHA-1 instead of the newer SHA-2 standard.
3. Ensure public facing software and hosting infrastructure is patched to current, and maintain vigilance in keeping it up to date.
4. Restrict physical access to credit cardholder data from employees, except those explicitly authorized to access it. Make sure the legitimate access to information is logged by user ID.

II. HIPAA

1. Enable Full Disk Encryption on all mobile devices with access to HIPAA compliant data.
2. Check the physical layout of monitors, computers and kiosks to ensure no un-authorized individuals can view or access HIPAA compliant data.
3. Design proper physical structure to protect the on premise equipment from theft or illegal access.

III. SOX

1. Identify all data classifiable as "business records" and create a plan to back up and archive it, along with any revisions made to the data. This could potentially mean scanning hand written documents into your network.
2. Hire an internal auditor to create and execute a plan to ensure all aspects of SOX are followed. Due to the complexity and broad scope of SOX, an internal auditor is essentially required to bring the business up to compliance. An external auditor is then hired to verify the work of the internal auditor. These auditors should work closely with IT to ensure nothing is left out of the security and compliance policy.

3. Create zones of access so employees only have access to what they need. An internal auditor should help to ensure these zones are properly in place and in use.

Good news, you made it to the end of the chapter! That wasn't so bad, was it? Now you are well on your way to ensuring your PCI/HIPAA/SOX compliant company is up to date and secured in a manner that makes you government-friendly AND ensures your data is safe and secure.

About Nick

For over 25 years, Nick Espinosa has been on a first name basis with computers. By the time he was twelve, he was building computers and programming in seven different languages. At fifteen, after achieving multiple tech certifications, he landed his first job in the IT field and at nineteen founded Windy City Networks, Inc. After 15 successful years, and numerous compliance certifications, Nick joined forces with BSSi2 as the CIO and Chief Security Fanatic in 2013.

As an expert in security and network infrastructure on every platform, Nick has consulted with clients ranging from a few computers to the Fortune 100 level. He has designed, built, and implemented multinational networks, encryption systems, and multi-tiered infrastructures as well as small business environments. He is passionate about emerging technology and enjoys keeping current by creating, breaking, and fixing test environments.

An industry thought leader, Nick is sought after for his advice on the future of technology and how it will impact every day businesses and consumers. Nick is a public speaker and has been quoted in *Forbes, American Express, CIO, EnterpriseTech, ITWorld, ComputerWorld, Solutions Review, InfoSec, CSO* and other publications regarding various technology and business leadership topics. He is also a columnist for *SmartFile,* writing regularly on security, technology and the future.

You can connect with Nick at:
- Email: nespinosa@bssi2.com
- Twitter: @NickAEsp
- LinkedIn: /in/nickespinosa
- SmartFile: smartfile.com/blog/author/nespinosa/

CHAPTER 16

STRENGTHENING BUSINESSES WEAKEST LINKS
– WHY EMPLOYEES NEED CYBERSECURITY TRAINING

BY PETER HOREWITCH,
Common Knowledge Technology

A business cannot thrive in today's world without having employees who understand the risks and concerns of cybersecurity.

Business owners are typically very vested in their employees receiving the proper types of training to help the business be more successful, and its employees become better assets as a result. In today's culture, employers place great emphasis on important things such as customer service training, sexual harassment and discrimination prevention policies, and even have employees sign Acceptable Use Policies for their computer systems. This is fantastic, of course, but something is missing. **Where is the cybersecurity awareness training?**

Do you know what is one of the most valuable parts of a business? Many may guess an asset that you actually see—such as inventory or a building—but in reality, it is data. Data is worth a lot of money and that's why it needs to be protected. There are people out there who would like to take it for their own gain. Through making conversations about the necessity of cybersecurity awareness training a priority, we've begun to see better results and smarter decisions.

STRANGER DANGER!

Nothing motivates us quite like doing whatever it takes to protect our children.

There are key phrases out there like "stranger danger" that we emphasize to children every day. We want them to make smart decisions that help keep them protected, while understanding the dangers in this world in a kid-friendly way. **Many business owners think of their enterprises as their kids—they've worked hard to build them up, sacrificed a lot for their well being, and only want the best for them.** This is where the "stranger danger" concept can carry over to employees of the business.

Think about it... We teach children to look for danger by analyzing situations before they get into them. Do we encourage them to answer the door without knowing who is there? No! Now carry this over into the technology world. Technology has many doors, all used for specific purposes like storing data, sending correspondence, and performing the daily functions necessary for the business to thrive, just to name a few. It takes just one cybercriminal to find an open door, sneak in and wreak havoc. It doesn't take them long to sabotage a business to get what they want once they enter into its technology. One minute, a business is on a fast, successful, growth track, the next, it can be on the verge of bankruptcy because of a security breach. All of this can be avoided if we train employees to do the right thing.

A highly effective step that any business can take, starting today, to help their employees understand and participate in cybersecurity is:
Help them recognize that having access to data is much like having access to the keys for the door to the business. Furthermore, it's likely a bigger responsibility for them to be aware of than having an actual key to your physical building.

OUT WITH THE OLD—IN WITH THE NEW

As it turns out, you can teach an old hacker new tricks.

Many times we think that the world is changing so fast that it seems impossible to keep up with it—it's exhausting! Cybercriminals carry traits that most of us would consider "good" to do "bad", including:

ingenuity, intelligence, determination, and tenacity. Staying one step ahead of everyone else is something they thrive on, because it is how they profit. For example: if they try to gain entry into 1,000 doors and end up with access to 20, that provides them with enough money to earn a very decent living.

Once upon a time, attacks were done that would trick employees into providing passwords over telephones or even going directly to a business and pretending to be someone else, knowing that employees would have no reason not to trust them. Who would intentionally manipulate a computer system for their own gain, right?

Today, there are new styles of attacks that are based on social engineering—making it look like a trusted source has sent something to the employee directly. They even use their name, which makes it appear all the more legit. For example:

A hacker sends the accounting department an email from the CEO, properly addressing it to the accounting person by name. It goes to their email and looks like it came from the CEO's address. It could even be a legitimate internal email if his password was compromised. He asks them to send a wire out for $10,000.00 to a certain vendor (likely a new one) and attaches the information. The employee is not comfortable questioning the CEO, even if they think it's strange, so they send it. Boom! They just sent a hacker $10,000.00 and there is no way to get that money back—ever. It's gone. All of this would have been avoided with a simple phone call to verify the CEO requested the transaction —a call that any CEO or business owner should be glad to have an employee make.

Today, malware and ransomware are two additional threats that businesses should be concerned about, and they are not that easy to identify. It's a game that, as of this moment, hackers are still winning because employees keep opening the doors.

IDENTIFYING RISK BEFORE IT'S TOO LATE

In the military's approach to cybersecurity, every employee that touches technology must take part in awareness training. This is because they know that the smartest way to ensure the security systems put in place are not compromised is to make sure no employee is a weak link in their line of defense.

Unaddressed threats and weaknesses equate to vulnerability for a business. Criminals are relentless, leaving no stone unturned before they move on to the next business. They'll move on considerably faster if you haven't left open any entrances for them. Do you know the largest areas of risk for businesses? Here are the biggest ones that apply to nearly every business.

(i). Email
Email is one of the most vulnerable threats for a business, despite it being an important part of how most organizations take care of business. Through email, attackers can often catch unaware employees. They're moving along quickly, eager to get their work done and they are not thinking about someone (or malicious programming) to create problems for them. This happens because hackers know that many employees do not pay attention. They are hoping for it, actually.

(ii). Remote Data Access
Most employees can access company email or even documentations from remote locations using laptops, their cell phones, or even their home computer. It's a great concept for helping today's employees be more productive while offering them flexibility. However, without the right training it may come with a costly price, including common things such as: theft of intellectual property, gaining access to customers' confidential information, and identifying passwords and bank accounts of your business.

(iii). Unsecured "On Site" Data
With the numerous regulations out there to protect consumers from mismanaged PII (Personal Identifying Information), there are hefty penalties if data is stolen by a hacker. It can lead to identity theft, insurance fraud, damaged reputations (for both customers and business owners), and it does become a great burden both financially and emotionally. Just ask a medical healthcare professional about the importance of HIPAA and you'll see a look cross their faces that

lets you know how serious it is. Violations involving breaches where data is stolen can lead to stiff penalties and fines, imprisonment, and a business closing down. If you are lucky, you may only have to pay for the wasted time the employee couldn't work because their computer needed to be fixed.

How would you or your employees answer these questions? Never assume, because one false assumption can be all it takes to sabotage your financial well-being and reputation.

- Do you know how to spot a malicious link? And what method do you choose to open up a link that you are unfamiliar with?
- How do you approach an email with a well-known sender that seems out of place? Do you just assume that it's really from that person? How do you evaluate it to see if it's safe?
- When information verification is requested from vendors, how do you share that information with them? Do you gladly share it over the telephone, or choose a different method? Why?

Questions like this are great ways for business owners to gauge what their employees' knowledge level is when it comes to cyber security. And if you, the business owner, are not sure, it's always the smart solution to bring in the IT professionals. The very name of my business—Common Knowledge Technology—was chosen because we are focused on making important IT decisions easier for business owners and decision makers to understand. This means ensuring that employees are aware and making smarter decisions about cyber security.

NINE WAYS TO MAKE EMPLOYEES INTO CYBERSECURITY GUARDS

The more levels of protection you train employees on, the better your chances will be.

When I go into a business, it's a dream if I'm getting the call in a proactive manner to help them prepare. Instead, I usually get a call which would sound like this: "Peter, please get here ASAP! We've been hacked. I don't know what to do!" In the spirit of taking the "cyber bull by the horns," let's go over what IT professionals can help businesses implement to protect and strengthen their two greatest assets—their employees and their data.

1. Train employees how to spot dangerous links: if you hold your mouse over a link that wants you to click to log into something, but you see that the link doesn't actually go to that website, you may be looking at a potential risk.

2. Know what to do with a strange pop up box: Many viruses are disguised as pop up boxes trying to trick you into clicking on them and unleashing the virus. One of them even claims to be Microsoft technical support reporting a problem and to click on it to let the Microsoft technician into your computer to fix it. If one of those boxes pops up on a PC, don't try to close it by clicking on the X in the right hand corner. Even that is sometimes a trick. Hit ALT-F4 to close the window. If you accidentally clicked on it and realized your mistake afterwards, unplug your computer from the network to contain the damage and call your IT provider.

3. Know where to look up hoaxes: one of the most reputable sites that will tell you if something is legitimate or a scam is Snopes. Take advantage of this source. Many times these hoaxes will start with, "If you want to protect your computer here is a new data security program…" You are likely not going to be protecting your data—you'll be giving it away.

4. Create a strong password: follow the suggestions from IT professionals on creating strong passwords. And please—never write it down on a sticky note! Lock and load that password to your memory.

5. Learn the proper places to store data: USB drives are not the place to store data because they can fail and they can be stolen. Then what? Data should be kept on a password protected server that is regularly backed up—whether this server is on-site or in the cloud.

6. If you really (and I mean really) are compelled to open a suspicious email, use an alternate device. To work with situations like this, Common Knowledge Technology uses what we call a "sand box." It's a computer that is meant for opening up suspicious emails and testing what happens with them. And be aware, unless you unplug that device from the network first, opening it may not contain the damage to that sand box computer. If you are really in a bind, sometimes its better to open it on your phone. Many malicious emails will not open up properly on a phone, so it is a slightly less risky way to test for something suspicious and reduces your chances of inviting something malicious in.

7. Put two factor verification into place: this is simple and highly effective, requiring that you enter a password first and then go through a second verification. The second one could be an extra password or even a code that's sent to you via text. It helps to ensure that the intended party is receiving the correspondence.

8. Keep kids away from your business technology: many of the games out there that kids can download for free contain software that they are also installing onto your technology. It could be a virus, or just a nuisance. Have you ever had something new just start popping up after a download? If you have, be warned—it may be there to retrieve other data.

9. Make your cybersecurity measures easy to use: while us IT guys think it's flattering that everyone thinks we are geniuses, we definitely understand that checks-and-balances systems for IT security must be easy to understand and use. If they're not, people won't use them and they'll be rendered useless. We don't want that!

Even though your IT provider has put in effective passive protections such as firewalls and filters, just like your physical office building has locks on doors and a security system, having the added protection of a security guard (in this case, a cybersecurity guard) will have the hackers that got in quickly moving onto another target.

THERE'S STRENGTH IN COMMITMENT

All employees can work together for a business's greater good.

Just like the seat belt in the car can't help protect you unless you actually put it on, it doesn't take that much training and getting into these habits to dramatically decrease the chances of a virus or malware causing problems. Knowing your employees are not going to open that virtual door to your business when a stranger comes knocking keeps your business safe, your customer's data safe and makes your business stronger. Using the help of experts in these fields is the most effective way to ensure that everything is working as it should and that employees are aware and trained in the best safety practices for the technology they have access to.

ONE THING IS DEFINITE: it is a more affordable and positive process to be proactive with employee training than it is to have to make that urgent call that you've been compromised. If, by chance, a criminal is able to get through the fence (firewalls, etc.) and smash the window, sounding the alarm, make sure they are met with a security guard who can take it from there.

About Peter

Peter Horewitch founded Common Knowledge Technology in 2003 with the philosophy that technology decisions do not have to be difficult. With 20 years of technology consulting and IT support experience, Peter knows that business leaders can make the right technology decisions when your IT partner is focused on making sense out of technology and turning it into Common Knowledge.

Peter graduated from Drake University with a Bachelor's degree in Information Systems and Insurance. After various technology support roles in the insurance industry, Peter joined the IAIABC, a worker's compensation trade association where he worked on developing electronic data standards for the industry. In this capacity, he served on the American National Standards Institute EDI standards committee, helping to define the electronic standards for the Health Insurance Portability and Accountability Act (HIPAA). Peter then joined the University of Kansas Medical Center and became the project leader to extend their voice, data and video systems to remote campuses, helping medical students access resources while on rural rotations.

From there Peter joined FrontRange Solutions as their Technology Research Manager, providing strategic direction on how to incorporate emerging technologies into their product lines such as GoldMine, an award-winning contact management system. Peter also headed up the project that certified FrontRange's help desk product HEAT as ITIL compatible, the most widely accepted approach to IT service management in the world. Before incorporating Common Knowledge Technology, Peter was a Principal Consultant for All Covered where he acted as the project manager.

Today, as the President of Common Knowledge Technology, Peter leads a top Colorado IT services firm that has helped hundreds of businesses make better technology decisions. He is focused not only on industry best practices and providing world class IT support, but building on the concept of providing technology leadership to its clients. This impactful approach ensures that your technology is helping you to wow your customers and leave your competition in the dust.

CHAPTER 17

RANSOMWARE

BY ALDAN BERRIE

WHAT IS RANSOMWARE?

What do you envision when you hear of holding something or someone for ransom? Probably an action movie including the offspring of a millionaire, a princess waiting to be rescued by her prince, or even a convenience store holdup in which police must pay to ensure the safety of innocent customers and employees. But, within the past several years, ransom has come to have a completely different meaning to many computer users – especially those with valuable data stored on their device or network.

Ransomware has become an increasingly common form of cybercrime due to its profitability with relatively simple application. Ransomware is a type of malware described as "malicious software" that is designed to restrict access to a computer's data until payment is processed. While a financial payment or "Ransom" has always been the primary purpose for Ransomware, the types of infection have evolved substantially over the years including the symptoms, methods of infection and even the payment methods in which to remove the infection.

Given it's growing popularity and historical profitability, if you utilize a computer on a regular basis, you will likely encounter some form of malware in your lifetime. Ransomware is a relatively new form of infection in which a user's computer will display a variety of messaging claiming their computers have been compromised along with a request for payment to fix or unlock their systems. In exchange for payment, restored access to the victims' system and files is typically offered using some type of code or decryption key with which to unlock the currently inaccessible data. Unfortunately for many victims, even after payment of thousands of dollars, the restored access to their computers applications and files that was promised is sometimes never achieved.

THE HISTORY OF RANSOMWARE

In the late 1980's, the first documented occurrence of Ransomware utilized what is currently the most effective ingredient of Ransomware, encryption. And although the method of encryption used within the original Ransomware occurrence was later determined to be too simplistic and ineffective in nature, it established the presence of not only Ransomware but, one of the most effective methods of rendering a computer systems data temporarily inaccessible, paving the way for the primary purpose of Ransomware, to successfully extort money from unsuspecting computer users.

It wasn't until the mid 1990's that two well-known computer scientists and cryptographic specialists implemented the missing components of the previously inferior Ransomware, using a proof-of-concept infection that utilized a more complicated form of encryption known as public key cryptography. This was a key ingredient to enabling a Ransomware author to extort money in exchange for the promise to regain access to previously encrypted data. A little known fact is that this original exploit was actually successfully written to infect the Macintosh operating system. This cryptographic form of Ransomware did not resurface until mid 2005, where a number of variants were discovered with increasing levels of encryption schemes. However, this time they were targeted at the more prevalent Windows operating systems.

From 2010 to 2013 a number of Ransomware infections took an interesting turn, and instead of encrypting the victim's data, would simply lock out access to the operating system and data displaying a payment option on the screen in order to regain access to the system. These variants were short lived and in 2013, the use of encryption-based Ransomware returned and has remained the most successful and prominent form of Ransomware in circulation.

THE TYPES OF RANSOMWARE

The least damaging and most simplistic Ransomware programs simply display messages trying to deceive victims into believing their computers have been attacked, with payment being the main means of "fixing" their systems, often times coming in the form of malware which will induce pop-up displays or overwrite your default home page in your web browser with a custom message and display.

A much more serious kind of Ransomware freezes a victim's device, often demanding payment be made to regain access to their computer or data. These ransomwares infect devices through a Trojan program, which is either a worm or virus that infects a computer typically by enticing someone to click on a file. The term Trojan is utilized to describe the method in which the malware spreads. In this case, much like the method which the ancient Greeks utilized to conquer the city of Troy, these infections often present themselves as an enticing or useful email or application, luring the unsuspecting victim to "click" or install the necessary files that infect a system with Ransomware. A common example of this ransomware is known as the "FBI Virus", which is actually a ransomware Trojan that typically freezes a computer, displaying a screen which states it's a message from the F.B.I. or other highly regarded police service, claiming the victim's computer has been used to do illegal activities, from child pornography to having an unauthorized version of windows, but assuring both usage and legal immunity will be granted once a payment of usually several hundred dollars is made.

As of the time of this writing, the most serious forms of ransomware are programs which encrypt data as they infect a device. Once the data is encrypted, it's very difficult, and sometimes impossible, to decrypt without the decryption key which the Ransomware creator offers in exchange for payment.

Because of their illegal status, these programs utilize extremely secure, untraceable methods in which to accept payments. Most recently, bitcoin has emerged as the preferred payment method due to its anonymity.

RANSOMWARE AND THE DARK WEB

It is generally accepted that malware is used directly by its developers. However, in many instances, developers will sell their creations on the dark web to other criminals, with the more advanced and prosperous programs raking in the highest revenue. Therefore, this illegitimate business is highly competitive and developers are always striving to create more advanced malware, causing it to evolve rapidly. The successes of Cryptolocker is a prime example of this competitive evolution in the ransomware world.

More recently, on June 23rd of 2015, the FBI released a public service announcement stating that between April 2014 and June 2015, the IC3 received 992 CryptoWall-related complaints, with victims reporting losses totaling over $18 million due to ransomware alone. The financial success of these encryption-based tools for extortion prove that the marketplace for Ransomware has grown significantly and shows no signs of slowing. More recently, an even more aggressive infection vector known as a "drive by" infection has emerged. A "drive by" infection occurs when you simply visit a website or advertisement that scans your pc in the background for an unpatched application, and then attempts to infect your system by exploiting any known vulnerability for that unpatched application. Here is a method of infection that does not even require someone to engage with or "click" on the infectious content from the website or advertisement.

HOW TO ELIMINATE RANSOMWARE ONCE INFECTED?

There are a few ways to rid yourself of different types of ransomware without paying a fee to criminals. To avoid paying unnecessarily, the first step is to be able to identify the type of malware. If a website has a banner, or another webpage opens displaying a warning about your computer, it is likely not legitimate. Additionally, if there's a popup claiming that your computer is in some sort of danger, chances are it's also illegitimate and potentially attempting to lure you into performing an action, such as clicking on a message, in which to further infect your system. If you suspect that you're a victim of ransomware or any form of malware, the first step to take is to disconnect your system from the network by physically unplugging the network cable connection and turning off your wireless network connection (the method for this depends on your system make and model). This is particularly important if you are connected to a network where other computers or data reside as your system could be causing damage to the other systems on the network without your knowledge. The next step is to contact your IT department and/or IT service provider and notify them of the symptoms that you have witnessed in order for them to investigate and remediate the issue.

Many times, a less advanced form of ransomware can be cleaned using one of the many available malware-removal applications and tools. A few that we have had success with include Sophos' virus removal tool, Sophos' Hitman Pro, Microsoft's Malicious Software Removal Tool and Malwarebytes Anti-Malware. When searching for a removal tool, perform the action from a healthy non-infected system and be sure to go with a reputable company. Stick with one of the security vendors mentioned here, or another that you have worked with in the past, and ensure that when downloading the resource, you do so directly from that company's website in order to avoid scams.

Removing ransomware in which your entire computer is frozen is more difficult. You would first need to recruit a separate computer system in which to utilize for downloading or copying removal programs through, as your currently infected system will not be very cooperative once infected and, if you recall our first step mentioned previously, you were to disconnect the suspected system immediately upon realizing that it may be infected. Assuming the infected system is running Microsoft Windows, first steps to resolve are typically to restart the infected computer in "safe mode". The goal here is to prevent the Ransomware programs from getting the opportunity to take over your system by running infectious processes upon startup. If able to boot the original system into safe mode, you will need to source a removal tool from a reputable security vendor (see above for references). Unless your IT provider already possesses one, the removal tool will typically need to be downloaded from the Internet. Again, the removal program should be retrieved from the security company's actual website as opposed to a third party website or blog.

Once downloaded to the alternate "healthy" system, the removal program would need to be copied over to the infected system using either USB, CD or DVD media and then run on the infected system, ensuring the instructions provided by the removal tool for cleanup are followed. It may also be possible to use a bootable removal tool, which would need to be utilized to boot the infected computer and then attempt to remove the offending malware. Currently, the most common media utilized for this purpose is a USB drive, CD or DVD that could be placed into the infected computer and booted from, as an alternative to the infected installation of Windows.

The safest method in which to clean a system that has become infected with malware is to restore from a backup. In this case, you would simply choose a restore point from a healthy point in time, prior to the infection. This assumes that you or your IT Provider has a regularly scheduled image of your system, applications and data from which to restore. There are many solutions that allow for this type of recovery however, this would need to be in place prior to the infection in order to be utilized, and there is no way to put this in place post infection for use in this effort.

If all else fails, you may wish to pay the ransom. We do not recommend this however, as there is no guarantee of encryption or infection removal, the payment process typically requires bitcoin currency, which can be difficult to acquire, and lastly, you are simply perpetuating the source of your frustrations by funding the creators of the infectious program that caused the issue to begin with.

WAYS TO PROTECT YOURSELF FROM RANSOMWARE

There are a number of measures in which to ensure effective levels of protection against ransomware. Many of these measures require an understanding of the underlying technology in order to fully utilize them. However, one of the most effective measures is the least technical in nature.

The first, and most effective way to prevent ransomware infections, is awareness. Education regarding what behaviors and actions represent different levels of risk, and how to reduce that risk, is the most important step to maintaining a healthy and productive technology ecosystem that is free of ransomware. Some fundamental methods in which to establish proper awareness is through the use of written company policies, educational materials (interactive tests, videos and written guidance) and follow-up testing. At Superior Solutions, we first establish a clients' technology use policy which acts as a guideline regarding appropriate use of technology resources.

The next step is to begin educating through the use of videos and written guidance for security best practices along with follow-up testing to determine each individual's level of understanding and absorption of security best practices. This can provide unlimited value and insight into whom might need some more guidance to remain safely inside of a company's risk tolerance. At the time of this writing, 91% of all successful data breaches began with a spear-phishing attack. This is simply a targeted email where an attacker sends an email to someone, usually faking the source of the email by impersonating someone that you regularly receive emails from, in order to get you to click on an attachment or download a file.

Once you click on the file or attachment, the infection has already begun, and all efforts to prevent cybercrime and data loss are essentially at risk. To mitigate this risk, Superior Solutions will send periodic phishing tests to see if any of our clients "bite" by clicking on them, download them or respond to them in any way. Anyone that fails the phishing tests is provided additional education and guidance to ensure that they are more aware of what to look out for, so as to avoid remaining a security liability for themselves and their employer.

Another layer of prevention can be implemented by way of the technology itself including but not limited to, the following:

1. A Firewall – Key features include advanced web filtering, SSL filtering, Anonymizer blocking, Country blocking and Tor traffic blocking.
2. Email Filtering – Filter out commonly known attachment culprits such as .exe, .zip, .rar, .cab, .scr, .bat, .cmd, .com, .ocx, .reg, .scr.
3. Ad Blocking – Typically a web browser plugin/extension.
4. Predictive Intelligence – Advanced level of predictive intelligence such as opendns.
5. Mobile Device Filtering – Remote agent-based web filter to protect against unsafe Internet connections including cafes, conventions and sometimes home networks.
6. Windows Security Patching – Managed updates for all systems.

7. Third Party application patching – Including Adobe reader, Java Runtime and Adobe Flash Player to name a few.
8. Third Party Applications – Tools such as CryptoPrevent may prove useful for locking down end-user devices to prevent infection.
9. Group Policies – Typically utilized to restrict systems on a network in order to prevent unauthorized applications from running, such as Ransomware.
10. Backup Solution – A backup solution with offsite storage is critical for recovery with today's business networks.

About Aldan

Aldan Berrie leverages over 20 years of experience in security, network infrastructure and application technologies to eliminate business process inefficiencies for small businesses, using the proper mix of technology solution identification, design and implementation. He and his team then deliver an ongoing support model for all technology resources, allowing small businesses to focus on their core competencies, as opposed to focusing on the technology solutions that enable them.

After graduating from the University of Georgia with a BBA in Management Information Systems, Aldan spent over 12 years designing and managing security and infrastructure solutions for Fortune 500 companies native to his hometown of Atlanta, GA, deciding to become obsessed with an even bigger challenge of delivering the same caliber of enterprise solutions to small businesses on a small business budget.

Aldan is the Founder and Director of Technology Solutions for Superior Solutions LLC, an Atlanta-based Outsourced IT Support and Managed Service Provider founded in May of 2000. Aldan is a Microsoft Certified Specialist with a focus on security, systems networking and cloud architectures. Aldan's mission is to establish the most respected IT Solutions provider through the consistent implementation and management of IT Solutions that accomplish specific, measurable profitability improvements through the proper leverage of technology for every small business.

You can connect with Aldan at:
- ab@superiorsolution.com
- https://www.linkedin.com/in/aldanberrie
- https://twitter.com/aldanberrie
- https://plus.google.com/+AldanBerrie

CHAPTER 18

IT SECURITY
– TARGETING AND INVESTING WISELY

BY SIMON FONTAINE

Security is important to you and in order to protect your business, you've probably put in place all the recommendations that have been suggested to you following the security audit that you've paid good money for. **However, if you have not followed the steps outlined in this chapter, you've probably missed that point and are not better protected today.**

Here's why. . .

The way in which security is typically approached is too general and does not take into consideration what is of the utmost importance for YOUR business.

For the past 15 years, here's what I've observed when performing Strategic Business-IT Planning for various business owners.

1. What needs to be secured is different from one business to another. So why then are audits performed with the same approach from business to business? And why do we recommend the same solutions to all clients?
2. What needs to be secured is never identified, and its value, if lost, is often not well estimated.
3. This information is generally not well communicated to the person

responsible for your network security. Knowing this, how can we have accurate security audits that target the essentials?

The essential information that is to be secured must come first and foremost from management and must be clearly communicated to the person(s) responsible for network security. We must leave no room for error or miscommunication. This approach must remain simple and you should NOT have to pay for copy/paste results.

After reading this chapter, here's what you'll gain:
- Why the approach outlined in this chapter is better suited to your business.
- You'll have the assurance that your business is better secured.
- You'll have the proof that the work is well done.
- You'll avoid paying unnecessary costs for general solutions and will be able to invest in what's really important for your business.
- You'll have the guaranty that the security level requested will be constant throughout the year—the lack of rigor being a well-known weakness in IT.
- You'll have a simple, easy-to-follow tool in the form of a canvas, efficient and easy to use.

The following five examples are from actual client meetings. They might surprise and help convince you.

Case #1
Security as seen by the president and owner of several retail stores...

"The most important document to secure is without a doubt the spreadsheet containing all the alarm codes to access each store."

Here, we understand the importance of this one particular file. Even with the best of intentions and the best technical resources, it's certain that an audit wouldn't have done any good here because this little piece of (critical) information had not been taken into consideration.

Case #2
Priceless data...

It's only after doing the exercise of trying to identify what's of value to the enterprise that a business owner realized that information contained in a database was worth an estimated five million dollars, and that if lost, this information could not be recovered. This information of a personal and confidential nature was coupled with a conversion table that allowed individuals and their information to remain anonymous. This table is the link between a person and their personal information.

After verification, the database and the conversion table weren't secured, nor backed up, and very few people even knew of the existence of this information.

Case #3
A lifetime's work on a USB drive. . .

While in a meeting with my client, I was surprised to find out that his work of more than 30 years was saved on a USB drive that the president of a manufacturing company kept in his shirt pocket. He proceeded to tell me that, if he lost that one drive, he'd have to shut his business down.

He even insisted that all other information (financials, HR information and price lists) were of no importance to him compared to that one single little device.

After verification, the information contained on that thumb drive was not even encrypted, password protected...or even backed up!

Case #4
Online orders worth their weight in gold. . .

This example is taken from a business that designs high-end vehicle graphics for fleet vehicles, buses and trailers.

Clients place their orders using their unique online service. The president's mains preoccupation is to block access to company data, price lists and client information. All efforts are geared towards that.

Case #5
A reflection that turns up money for a business. . .

Several months after implementing a Strategic Business-IT Plan for a manufacturing business, the general manager informed me of one particular piece of machinery that's highly crucial to his business. He insisted that if this equipment were to fail, his entire production would stop.

He proceeded to tell me that all his clients personal settings and configurations were digitally stored on that one machine. He was referring to a robot paired to a 6-year-old computer for which only the support people located in Germany have the key to access this information. After verification, there was no backup or protection on this equipment.

This information was brought up thanks to reflection and awareness on security during a Strategic Planning meeting. I did, in fact, notice that even several months after reflecting on this, people remain alert, attentive and sensible to what's really important to their business. **It's from this perspective that security must be addressed.**

What's valuable to a business is subjective. Your business is unique, especially it's security. Most security audits don't reach the desired goal. Consequently, you're paying good money for results that are not custom tailored to your needs and often miss the goal of securing what's most important.

Here's how most audits* are performed:
- Inspection of your backups
- Update antivirus and scan for viruses
- Internal and external intrusion detection
- Check for patches and updates
- Validation of network admins allowed in your network
- Validate repertory security

*Please note that this list is used only as a reference to show what is usually done while performing a security audit. *If the auditor is not made aware of what really matters to your organisation, it simply won't be taken into consideration and the audit will be useless and incomplete.*

Of course it's important to address the items listed above and to neglect nothing. However, the goal is not to secure everything, but to find the proper balance. You don't want to be as secure as the NSA (National Security Agency); that wouldn't make sense...**Target what's important and make sure nothing is forgotten.**

Here's how:

Step 1: Implicating upper management

Firstly, at your next management meeting, ask each member what is the most important information they want secured and what is the value of this information to your business in case of loss. This simple exercise will take only five minutes and you may be surprised at the answers. Take notes. You will certainly hear different perspectives, one equally as important as the other. You might be surprised at what you can discover!

Now, do you have 100% certainty that your organization is well protected?

Secondly, put aside one hour at your next meeting for a more elaborate discussion. I can assure you of one thing: it will be of great service to your business if everyone in management participates in this process. Each and every member has pertinent information to share that you might not be aware of. You have everything to gain. Technology plays an even more important role in business. So this will be an hour very well invested. We are talking about the continued existence of your business here.

You should take the time to perform this exercise and make sure that this meeting is productive and useful. Do not hesitate to ask for help. Your IT consultant should be able to assist you. **It is very difficult to put a price on the value of your data,** but you should insist on this because once you've put a price on what's important, it's easier to know how much to invest.

Peace of mind, eliminating all doubt and knowing that everything has been put in place to protect your business and your client's data is what you want. Surprises are not always a good thing. . .

Step 2: Identifying what's to be protected (Sensitive Data and Critical Services)

Of course, you must protect yourself from data loss, but hackers also look to make your business inoperable (denial of service) by targeting your IT infrastructure.

There are two types of attacks:

- Category 1 : An attack that is meant to steal or destroy business data (sensitive data)
- Category 2 : An attack that's meant to disrupt or interrupt a company's operation (critical services)

Here are some examples:

Category 1: Sensitive data
- Price lists
- Confidential employee or client information
- Intellectual property (recipes, plans, drawings)
- Payroll documents

Category 2: Disruption or interruption of a company's critical services (IT services and processes)
- Production-oriented software (for example, your ERP software and database)
- POS (Point Of Sale) Software
- Credit Card processing

I've put together an IT security template to make this easier. (See next page for IT Security template.) It will help bring out the essential elements of the two categories and indicate their criticality level and asses the financial impact. This IT security template will become an important reference point. It will act as a work tool to be used in audits, management follow-ups, critical maintenance evaluation of security processes put in place and to make sure to avoid any confusion to assure that the responsible resource people take charge. This IT security template will assure the success of this process. (IT security template website info. in bio.)

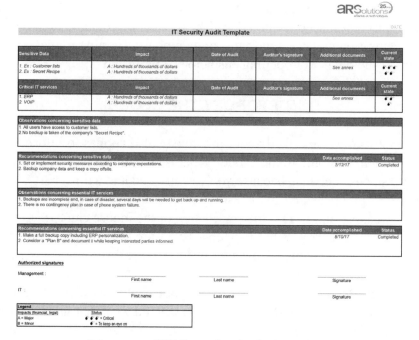

Diagram of IT Security Audit Template.

We quickly come to the conclusion that this exercise will give different results from one company to another. The goal of this more personalized approach has the advantage of helping guide the verifications in order to avoid unnecessary costs with audits that are just a cut-and-paste of other business audits. I must point out that the involvement of management in this exercise is a must. Your business will come out a winner!

Step 3: The audit and upgrade corrections

Once the IT security template is completed, an audit will give management the cold, hard facts about the current state of the targeted elements. It should explain the upgrade if necessary and the costs related to it.

Step 4: Maintenance and follow ups

The key to success resides in rigorous security maintenance and follow ups. **This is often a neglected aspect in IT, we should pay more attention to it.** In addition to performing regular audits (once or twice a year), it is essential that we incorporate these verifications into our monthly maintenance routine.

It's important that I point out that the approach outlined here should, in no way, replace best security practices like regular scheduled maintenance, virus definition updates and scans, and employee training to make them aware of the danger of opening suspicious emails, etc.

DON'T FORGET THE CLOUD!

The approach we've talked about previously also applies to information you might have stored in the Cloud. What is essential and critical to your business doesn't change because you've entrusted it to a third party. Even using best practices and the latest technology, human error will always be the weakest link in IT. One small click of the mouse can bypass even the strongest security. What happens if you are without access to your data and/or applications for days, or even worse, everything is lost?

What is included in your contract with your cloud provider? Review in detail what's included and what's not. Go beyond what that sales guy told you and read it carefully to make sure you understand it. It's better to be safe than sorry. Wouldn't you want to find out now before it's too late?

IN CONCLUSION

In addition to simplifying, reducing costs and making the approach to business security a more effective one, the process described here is a more personalized one adapted to your business reality, which is the desired result.

About Simon

For the past 27 years, Simon Fontaine and his team have been helping to bring peace of mind to business owners in the fields of manufacturing, professional services and point of sale when it comes to their IT environment. President and Founder of Les Services Informatiques ARS Inc., a company that specializes in Strategic IT Business Planning, Integration and Infrastructure Management for Quebec City area's businesses, Simon is also a best-selling author for his collaboration in: *The Business Owner's Essential Guide To I.T. and All Things Digital – Vol. 2 – 17 critical facts every business must know to maximize their company's efficiency, security, employee productivity and profit.*

With more than 27 years of experience under his belt in the IT Business World, Simon has acted as a consultant to business owners and CEOs in order to help them use technology strategically to achieve their business goals. For Simon, technology must contribute to a business's success, deliver results and simplify tasks. Not to invest more, but invest differently. Simon has built a process that allows him to guarantee 100% results if it's followed precisely or the client doesn't pay. He adds to his experience specific tools acquired throughout the years combined with target indicators and measurables adapted to each business's reality.

To explain his strategy, Simon" has been invited on several occasions to share his expertise on "PME en Action" (Businesses in Action), a well-known business and financial TV show on TVA's "Canal Argent" (Quebecor Media, an important broadcaster in Canada). Simon is also a seasoned contributor to several magazines and blogs in the province's business community.

Founded in 1989, ARS accounts for more than 300,000 interventions and projects throughout the Province of Quebec in businesses ranging in size from 50 to 1000 employees. ARS has a proud reputation of being able to take on any IT-Business challenger and deliver results.

You can get in touch with Simon at:
- simon.fontaine@ars-solutions.ca

To view the IT security template discussed in Step.2:
- www.ars-solutions.ca/itsecuritytemplate

CHAPTER 19

SEVEN STEPS YOU NEED TO TAKE TODAY TO SECURE YOUR COMPANY AGAINST CYBERCRIMINALS

BY MICHAEL C. SKOMBA

Cybercriminals steal data from you and your company. They are not the sophisticated genius types you see on television or the movies – they are thieves and extortionists, plain and simple.

Not nice people like you and me.

They hijack system resources and hold them for ransom. Some are just vandals or pranksters and just annoying, but others use malware, guesswork or deception to exploit your networks. Worms and viruses arrive hidden in seemingly friendly attachments – and then they wreak havoc, often immediately, but sometimes they bide their time for a better time to strike. Trojan horses launch spyware or exploit vulnerable ports. Keylogging software is used to track your typing of passwords and other important data, while the Phishers snag your data using spoof emails and sham web sites to do the same. Packet sniffers grab it in transit. Silently, Rootkits force 'zombie' computers to send spam or stage denial-of-service attacks, unbeknownst to their owners. Other use low-tech schemes, such as cracking passwords by trial and error or making crank calls to helpdesks to obtain passwords and other useful information, and that is often as effective as their more sophisticated cousins in the world of Cybercrime. To make matters worse, their methods are openly touted and shared or sold on less-than-respectable file sharing websites.

Oh Boy! What ever happened to keeping the bad guys out just by locking our stuff in a room?

According to the Small Business Association's Statistics of U.S. Businesses, there are about 28 million Small-to-Medium Businesses (SMB's) in the U.S., two-thirds of which contributed about $7.5 trillion to the U.S. economy.

This makes SMB's both lucrative and heavily targeted victims for Cybercriminals. Even more so because many of these businesses are unaware of what is at risk, and what they need to do to secure their companies IT infrastructure.

A study from the National Cyber Security Alliance stated that, "36 percent of cyber-attacks were conducted against SMBs. Of those, up to 60 percent went out of business within six months of an attack. Yet 77 percent of SMB owners still believed their companies were safe from cyber-security breaches according to the same study."

Addressing this apparently false sense of security, Andrew Grove, former CEO of Intel's Insight shares his thoughts that, "Success breeds complacency. Complacency breeds failure. Only the paranoid survive."

In another study, the National Small Business Association (NSBA) found that, "The average direct cost to a small business for a single attack was almost $9,000, excluding brand damage and other soft costs. Also, SMBs incur nearly four times the per capita cybercrime costs of larger firms."

How did we get here? I know, just writing this I'm feeling more and more paranoid… are you? Is someone reading every word I'm typing and laughing at me? I hope not!

Let's start by looking at the Internet and how technology has become ingrained in our everyday lives. All our personal and business communications in almost every way is digital - whether we want it to be or not. Our email, our social media, bookkeeping, documents and even our phones have become entombed in devices, applications, apps and the digital data we access and use, but all the while most of us have little idea of how the technology actually works. We just like all the cool stuff we can do with technology and how we can do it quickly and efficiently. But for all the good this technology brings to our work and our lives, we have to recognize that there is a darker, seamier side. The growing attempts of organized cybercriminals to further their illicit activities leaves us wondering, "How do we stay connected and protect our companies, our data, our assets and our reputation?"

"2015 was a particularly bad year for hacks and computer intrusions, and it looks like 2016 will only get worse." . . . according to a recent report by the antivirus software manufacturer, Panda Security. "In fact, more than a quarter (27 percent) of all malware samples ever recorded were produced in 2015. . . and our Lab researchers detected and disabled more than 84 million new samples of malware in 2015 — 9 million more than the previous year."

What this means is that cybercriminals were churning out new malware samples at a rate of more than 230,000 per day throughout 2015, and the numbers are growing.

It's seems that every few days there is a new headline talking about another company or institution being breached by hackers. It would seem logical that these organizations would have the funds and expertise to prevent these attacks from happening, so how come they fall prey to these attacks? Part of the reason is that. . . "Attacks are growing at 45% year-on-year globally," according to security firm Alert Logic, an industry leader in providing managed cloud security and compliance solutions.

These Cyber Criminals keep doing what they do simply because for them - it is low risk with high profits – and they can perpetrate their crimes from anywhere in the world with little interference from law enforcement.

So let's talk a little about the latest methods these cybercriminals are using to create havoc, and maybe then we'll understand how to better thwart their efforts.

A writer once asked a literary agent, "What kind of writing pays the most?" Her answer was simple - "Ransom notes."

That is why "Ransomware" is rapidly becoming one of the favorite income streams in the cybercrime world. CryptoLocker, CryptoWall, TorrentLocker and other variants of this nefarious type of malware, when introduced to a PC, a Mac or a Server will securely encrypt the user's file systems preventing any access to all data. Then the cybercriminal demands some form of payment to unencrypt them. Quite often there is a time limit to making payment before the data is destroyed, which makes it seem all the more dire to the infected party, who is even more prone to just "pay up" before all their data is lost. These Data-Pirates have several different methods to collect these ill-gotten gains, but the takeaway on this new cash cow for cybercriminals is: *No one is immune once successfully attacked, and you will pay the ransom or lose all of your data.*

Some companies employ the "head in the sand" approach to Cyber-security - "Our survey finds half of SMBs believe they are immune to targeted cyberattacks and fail to implement basic Internet safeguards." Says a Symantec SMB Threat Assessment Poll, "These same SMBs often believe they are too small for hackers to target, or that they have little of value that cybercriminals would choose to steal."

Cybercriminals, when they aren't busy denying access to or ransoming personal PCs and Macs, are doing much the same to a more lucrative target – SMB digital corporate assets – directly or through web sites and online storefronts. They are business savvy and realize that hacking personal resources equates to one target and one man's personal information, whereas hacking corporate assets equates to one target and many sources of valuable information – all for about the same effort on their part.

Since the beginning of electronic computing, cybercriminals have been trying to access information from employee and consumer computers – especially account numbers, credit card numbers and passwords for critical applications. This information allows them to assume someone's identity and use their credentials – and then they access a myriad of schemes to turn that information into cold, hard cash.

To combat cybercriminals, large corporations need large IT budgets and they employ highly-skilled, highly-trained and very well paid (read that as expensive) Security Experts. These security professionals engineer, monitor and maintain very complex security solutions to "lock" things down and try to prevent successful attacks from occurring. They know to expect a loss sooner or later, and they develop extensive contingency plans.

SMB's with smaller IT budgets and lacking a dedicated Security Expert on staff are finding it very difficult to gain the knowledge and expertise to effectively recognize or deal with the prevention of Cybercrime. Then there is the dilemma of, and surviving, a successful attack and dealing with the after-effects.

Below are seven steps you need to consider to help secure your company against cybercriminals:

1. Keep your operating systems and applications updated and regularly patched.

Many cyber-attacks are successful because of unpatched system vulnerabilities. Make sure your Operating System and Security patches are applied in a timely and universal manner.
The number one application to be attacked are your Web Browsers. For regular browsing, be aware of client-side vulnerabilities in your Web Browsers. For business "Line of Business" applications requiring a browser - contact your vendors regarding browser specific requirements and versions. Plan to invest some time into learning, selecting, installing and configuring all the security features for the browser you select. Your browser will need regular ongoing maintenance as the security features and settings change as the risks evolve.

Require monthly or quarterly reporting from your IT Professionals on what systems and applications have received updates and have been patched, as well as what has not and if not, the reasons why.

2. Use a firewall with solid UTM - Unified Threat Management.

A UTM Firewall integrates a wide range of security features into a single appliance. UTM appliances combine firewall, gateway anti-virus, as well as intrusion detection and prevention capabilities into a single platform. Use the embedded security features to lock down the ability of employees to use home PCs and BYOD's to access your network through Cloud applications. Lastly, restrict software downloads and set up and control administrative rights so that nothing can be installed on company-owned computers without proper authorization.

3. End-User Participation to maintain endpoint security is essential.

The statement, "The problem . . . is between the seat and the keyboard." is often cited as the major cause of many security breaches.

Social engineering is a non-technical method of intrusion that cybercriminals use which relies heavily on human interaction, and often involves tricking people into breaking normal security policies and procedures. It is one of the greatest threats that organizations encounter today.

Most operating systems and applications come with a reasonable amount of security policies in place. Unfortunately for convenience's sake or from lack of training, they are not used and are often circumvented.

Password Policies, usually the first line of defense, is the most neglected. Review and enforce features such as complexity, frequency of password changes. Everyone should know the importance of a strong Password Policy, both in business and personal computer use.

2-Factor authentication - In addition to a user name and password for user access, a secure code is texted to a smartphone and required to complete authentication - this should be employed whenever available.

Security policies need to be reviewed annually if not bi-annually with end-users, to ensure they are educated about things like the proper use and protection of Passwords, restricted access to corporate data and the risks associated with accessing corporate data from mobile devices.

An acceptable use policy (AUP) is a document stipulating constraints and practices that a user must agree to before gaining access to a corporate network or the Internet at work. Most businesses require that employees or vendors sign an acceptable use policy before being granted a network ID.

4. Anti-Virus and Anti-Malware Software.

The use of anti-virus and anti-spyware tools has long been trusted to provide adequate protection from attacks by viruses and malware. Unfortunately, the cybercriminals are constantly increasing their efforts to bypass each generation of these tools, and the manufacturers have to continually modify their products to detect and block the attackers in response to new threats.

There are a variety of Access-Permission solutions that are gaining popularity. They slow the flow of unauthorized applications from being installed and they should be considered as an additional tool in your arsenal for added protection.

Be sure to research and select only highly-rated solutions to maximize your protection.

Budget the time to apply definition updates. It is also suggested you re-evaluate the products you use annually at the minimum.

5. Use an Image-based Backup with Cloud Storage.

A cybercrime incident such as a malware infection or the hacking of your company's systems could result in the destruction or loss of important company data. Having a backup of all your data is essential for recovering from such an incident with the least possible interruption to your operations.

With image-based backups, a picture of the workstation or server's operating system and data is created in real-time and then stored as a place in time. This is essential for restoration because rebuilding or virtualizing a workstation or server requires not just the data files, but also the applications and operating systems to be restored as quickly and as up-to-date as possible, to be effective in keeping losses to a minimum.

When keeping copies of backups, consider that your company systems could have an undetected malware infection for a considerable period. Today, most quality image backup solutions provide some form of inverse chain technology that allows restoration from multiple points of time and over a longer time period. This is essential so you can restore to just before an attack was successful, saving considerable time and energy, and of course – income!

Additional advantages of image-based backup both locally and in the Cloud are: full restores are faster, as well as the ability to restore individual files, boot virtual machines, perform bare metal restores (BMR), and determine image integrity – and in a major security disaster, you can run your offices from a cloud datacenter if needed.

6. Protect your Bank accounts.

Everyone is doing some kind of banking or finances online today.

So first of all, start by cancelling your debit cards as they are the #1 way banking accounts are compromised and they generally offer little or no loss protection from the banks. The backing for debit cards is not some credit line, but your money.

The second way to prevent giving the bad guys your hard-earned funds is to use a dedicated PC for online banking and then DON'T use that PC for accessing any other web sites, email access, social media sites or for downloading files and applications. Some companies choose to use the same dedicated PC for online payroll as well as online banking which is considered acceptable.

Remember to change your password at least every 90 days and use very strong passwords. Always use 10 plus characters with random combinations of upper and lower case, numbers, characters and symbols.

Contact your bank and sign up for email alerts whenever a withdrawal over $100 happens, and require YOUR signature for any and all wire transfers.

Have your money spread out in multiple accounts to minimize the risk. Ask your bank what type of accounts offer what type of prevention and protection from Cybercrime, and evaluate your acceptable loss potential.

7. Buy Cyber Insurance.

After reading all this you probably have come to the conclusion that your business at some point in time will most likely suffer some kind of cyber-attack and there will be some kind of loss. So be prudent and meet with your business insurance broker and evaluate what dollar amount in damages or liability your business can afford, and make sure you get Cybercrime insurance for that amount, plus a little extra in coverage.

Make sure you know what your responsibilities are in proving a loss occurred, and how the valuation of that loss is established. Most insurance companies will provide a list of what items you will be expected to have in place to prove any losses from a cyber-attack were not due to negligence or carelessness.

An organization failing to exercise due diligence in securing its computers could be held legally liable for identity theft attacks against its employees, customers and vendors. Be sure your coverage addresses these liabilities.

Many business Insurance policies provide some kind of compensation for restoration of lost data. Make sure that amount reflects what you would need after a severe attack.

Many SMBs are outsourcing their cybersecurity to Managed Service Providers (MSPs) or Managed Services Security Providers (MSSPs) to make up for their lack of time and in-house expertise. Hiring a competent Managed Services Security Provider to help you develop an action plan is a good way to stay on top of securing your company. We are in a service economy and the commoditization of IT Services gives you access to the best and brightest for the management and security of your networks.

By outsourcing IT Services, you reduce or eliminate time-consuming operational burdens. Managed Service Providers ensure all devices have the latest software updates, maintain management and security updates for servers and workstations, and deliver solutions that leverage cloud-based architectures to give you the best IT has to offer.

SMBs no longer need to go it alone against Cybercriminals because through a mix of managed cybersecurity approaches and professional management outsourcing, they can deploy and maintain efficient cybersecurity and intrusion prevention as well as larger enterprises, and for a fraction of the costs.

About Michael

Michael Skomba relates to his clients as someone who has been on both sides of the fence. He started working with computers when his family service business first computerized 30 years ago. When he received the first invoice for computer support, he quickly realized the value in working with computers and proceeded to start a small side-venture focused on aiding other small businesses to transition into the computer age. It didn't hurt that he really enjoyed working with computers.

Michael learned about computers with self-study, online training and on-the-job experience. He studied at New Horizons Computer Learning Centers for Windows Server and successfully received his MCSE+I – the Microsoft Certified Systems Engineer + Internet accreditation.

In 1995, his company "The NIC Group" was started to specifically provide IT support for Small-to-Medium-sized Businesses. This company has grown and developed a wide base of professional, corporate and non-profit clients. Many of his original clients are still with the NIC Group 20+ years later. While concentrating on Network Management, Security Solutions and Cloud-Hosted solutions, the NIC Group helps SMB's do what they do best – Be Successful!

Michael is happily married, has two grown married children and 3 grandkids he adores. Always ready to go fly fishing, he also loves motorcycling and gardening. He is a co-author of, *HOW TO FIND THE RIGHT IT CONSULTANT.*

Michael is a member of ASCII, Comp-TIA and Truth@Work.

You can connect with Michael at:
- mskomba@NICG.com
- www.nicg.com
- www.facebook.com/nicgroupinc
- https://www.linkedin.com/in/michael-skomba

CHAPTER 20

YOU'VE LOST IT ALL. . . HOW QUICKLY CAN YOU RECOVER YOUR DATA?

BY SCOTT E. PALMQUIST,
Computer Support Team, Inc.

Every minute counts, from the hacking event to the actions that are taken.

Some people might believe that businesses focus on policy too much—that it's out of control to have policies for everything that "might" happen. There is such a thing as overboard, for certain. *However, there is one policy that should be in place in 100% of businesses of all sizes that use a computer for anything.* That is a **Disaster Recovery Plan (DRP)**. Without this document, a business can suffer dire consequences in an attack, including:

- Its insolvency
- Fines and penalties
- Serious uphill struggles to rebuild their reputation
- A return to profits
- Customer trust

One of those problems above is hard enough to overcome. *Can you even fathom trying to manage multiple problems at once, with employees that do not understand what needs to be done?* That is exactly what happens

193

to a business that is unprepared for an event where they lose their data, whether it is from hacking or equipment failure.

THE GOAL OF A DISASTER RECOVERY PLAN

Pinpointing and prioritizing what data and applications your business requires to be able to perform its most essential functions and educating everyone on a notification and recovery process is   the goal.

A DRP is a policy that has been put into place by IT professionals who understand how to contain, manage, and recover lost data, whether it is due to hacking, a cyber-security breach, user error, and/or equipment failure. For no explainable reason, server hardware can fail—with no warning at all! Things happen… **the true test is in how we respond.**

There are some bits of data that are more essential to recover than others. As a business owner, you must think about what is a "must have" for recovery as quickly as possible, compared to what is a second level priority. By doing this, you will already have taken a purposeful step toward pinpointing the order of operations should you lose your data. Imagine that you own a business that operates mostly during the week, but on weekends you have one employee who comes in. He's starting his shift on late Friday and he goes to open a file. He clicks on it. It opens, but something doesn't look quite right. It's infected! This employee has two choices on what to do next:

- (a). Quickly close that file and move on to the next thing, hoping that it was caught in time.
- OR
- (b). Refer to the DRP that he was trained on and go into "urgent action mode."

Far too many employees go with Answer (a). And why? Because there is no Answer (b) in place. Instead of getting to work on containing the malware that is ready to cause serious troubles, they may just try to forget about it, or say, "I'll bring it up on Tuesday when I have to go to the office."

We've seen this happen to multiple businesses that would not take our advice on creating a DRP and would not setup proper backups. The employee at one particular client found their data was encrypted by ransomware on a Friday night, around 7 PM. He did not notify anyone until his next shift on Wednesday. The company lost five years of data, including data on other computers in the same location. If the employee would have notified the appropriate person, the ransomware could have been stopped before infecting other computers and critical data.

It's a partnership between a DRP and employees and IT. Each needs the other to be effective in helping a business make it through an event. People get stressed and rattled in times of crisis when they feel ill-prepared. The DRP is what helps everyone come together and work as a team to do what they can.

CREATING A DRP

When everyone knows what they should do and how the process of data recovery will go, everyone can better work together to solve the problem and recover what was lost.

To ensure that everything is covered in creating a Disaster Recovery Plan, you must go into great detail and come up with systems and solutions that are tested and proved for recovering the lost data. **Tested and proved** is key here. *Just writing something down without actually putting it to the test to see if it works becomes nothing more than a theory or an educated guess.* Not very comforting "in the heat of the moment," is it?

There are no less than 14 factors which are included in a DRP. Each one is discussed in a way that is "business specific," meaning that it is focused on your business and how you run. It's not a generic blueprint; it's a finely-tuned policy that tells everyone in a business' organization, as well as their IT partnership, exactly who is doing what and when. Many of these tasks fall on the IT guy, which is why the partnerships that I create with my clients are so important. We are on the same team!

Whether you have a DRP in place at this time or you now realize how essential it is to create one, look through these eight points and put some thought into how well trained your entire organization is in dealing with a disastrous data loss.

1. Expectations of employees
By giving employees the proper training and knowledge about what

the consequences are of data loss for the business (a/k/a keeping their jobs, possibly), you can build a supportive, efficient team that knows what to do. Think of the mother that knows how to get all the kids on the same page when they get bickering—your employees can all become that. Because keep in mind, disasters don't happen only when the few select trained people are working. They happen any time.

2. Creating the best backup possible for business' individual situation

Of course all businesses cannot afford large corporation-level backup, but they should do what they can do, either budgeting it in for future goals, or else making adjustments to implement it ASAP. You never want to be a "day late" for this, because by not being proactive, you'll find that the recovery process is considerably more costly. It's a lot more work and man hours and lost revenue. According to a determined budget, file-based backup technologies, applications and services configuration backups, operating systems backups, BDR backups, and even failover server backups can be determined.

3. Determining what needs to be backed up

While determining what needs to be backed up and how frequently, you want to consider what data is the most important to recover first. This data will be pertinent to:

- The business being able to perform its most essential functions
- Preventing long term damage due to both loss of revenue and non-ability to perform

Some businesses are okay with it taking a day or two to get certain data recovered. The DRP will factor in how the most pertinent data is the priority. You need to consider:

- How much data can you afford to lose? Is it one day, one hour, fifteen minutes?
- How long do you need to go back to recover data? Is it one year, five years, seven years? There are many regulations and requirements that mandate what a company must save, or risk penalties as a result.
- Do you know exactly what all your industry's requirements are as the business owner? You need to know what the exact

consequences are for retaining data and protecting it; especially your customers' data.

4. Define data and applications

Define which data and applications are critical for your business, as well as how long you can go without having access to them. For example, while creating a DRP for one of our clients we determined they had a "mission critical" application they could not function without, so we setup a BDR backup for that server. On a Saturday morning at 8:07 AM, the server crashed. Because of the DRP, and the BDR backup, we had the server up and running in 21 minutes from an 8:00 AM backup, with no data loss. Most employees didn't even know the server went down.

5. Files and file locations

Knowing where every server file, workstation file, NAS (Network Attached Storage) file is must be a part of the DRP. Knowing where to look and locate all data is an intricate part of the recovery process. Knowing how often all data is backed up is also a part of this process. With the popularity of Cloud syncing now, we also need to ensure that we are taking that into account. The Cloud now makes it possible for files to be on a server and also in the Cloud. We work with clients to create a DPR that will determine if they need to have both back-up plans in place for individual work stations, individual emails only, or the entire Cloud. Through this collaborative effort we also train the employees about the entire process.

6. Operating system details

All the information about the server(s) and router(s) that a business has are a part of this step, which means the server services configuration backup (i.e., DHCP, DNS, Active Directory, etc.). By configuring and completely setting up the back-ups, we can ensure that all server service configurations are set up properly, which is very important if there is no full image backup in place. With a full image backup all data can be restored to its most recent level. This is necessary to completely restore a system and its data to 100%.

Two important parts of this step are:
- Knowing that the file-based backup can also be compressed and encrypted, to further protect data. This is particularly

important if the data loss is from cybercrime and not equipment error.

- Implementing the proper employee training and safeguards for all BYOD (Bring Your Own Device) data. Pay particular attention to employees who work with high levels of sensitive data in this step.

7. Determining the exact order of the backup plan

You've determined a lot and together with your IT expert, you've addressed everything that is taken into account with recovering lost data. Now it is time to put all of this information into an outline and plan of action. Essentially, this becomes the manual that tells everyone—employees, business owner, and IT personnel—what needs to be done and in what order. It factors in priorities, locations of all devices and technologies, and assures that the business has "dotted the i's and crossed the t's" for their DRP.

8. Test your plan

The time to test your DRP is not when you are relying on it to get your business back up and running. It is *absolutely necessary* to do trial runs and tests to see if it will work. This will help give peace of mind, as well as the opportunity to make tweaks to make for a better DRP. Here are some questions that I ask my clients to consider so they can be factored into considering what should all go into the schedule for testing the plan and how frequently:

- *Do you see any technology updates taking place in the near future?* If you are making constant changes, additions, and adjustments to technology, the plan will need to be tested more. At a minimum—it can be spot tested with a focus on the new technologies.
- *How much employee turnover do you have?* This is important because having even a few employees untrained on how to handle their role in a significant data loss can be costly. While you may not have to perform an entire system run-through, you should focus on continuing education and training for employees about the steps that need to be taken. Also…if an employee leaves that plays a role in managing or participating in the DRP, the replacement needs to know everything as quickly as possible. Going through a test run is a very effective, hands-on way to ensure that they are comfortable with the process

and understand the expectations.

- *Are any regulations that are industry standard for your business adjusting?* As certain regulations change that regard Internet security, cybercrime, and customer data requirements, you want to make sure that you are complying with those. It can even be a soft marketing source of comfort for businesses to let their customers know that their information is of the utmost importance to the business.

For businesses that do not typically fall into the parameters listed in the above questions, it is suggested that you test and tweak (as necessary) the DRP on an annual basis. And after that—make sure everyone has access to the most recent copy of the plan—in paper form—and knows that it is there. Give any additional training on updates to the plan that may be necessary.

YOU'VE GOT THIS!

Your business now has an edge. Knowing that there is a way to return a business to full function at a rapid pace after a data loss event will give you an advantage.

Computer Support Team, Inc. (CST) is passionate about helping businesses to understand what is necessary to protect the data that is so intricate to their livelihood. Through our partnerships with our clients, we are able to create effective Disaster Recovery Plans that help give our clients peace of mind. **If the "undesirable" happens and there is a data loss event, we are able to jump right into action and resolve the problem more rapidly and restore all data quickly—much quicker than we can without a plan.**

Your business data is not something that should be left to chance. It should be protected the best way possible for the sake of both the business and its customers. **In a world where time flies by for many people, don't encourage it to stop and drag on due to the stress of a data loss.** It's time to organize a DRP to better protect your business and know you can recover your data quickly and get back to business.

About Scott E.

Scott E. Palmquist helps businesses leverage technology to help their productivity and bottom line. Back in the days of DOS he was an 'At Home' Dad. "It was great to be able to make the choice to stay home with our son." His musician days (as a drummer) were over and he sold his new and used compact disc store to stay home with his son. To keep his mind, and entrepreneurial spirit, alive, he traded his drum set in for a computer. He spent the next few years helping friends and family with every tech issue and need. Eventually, his wife's employment situation changed and they decided it was her turn to stay home with their son.

Enter Microsoft Certification. Scott E. went to a great Microsoft Certification training center with amazing instructors. After a year of hard work and great hands-on experience, he had a business. Through referrals, his business grew quickly. He still supports his very first client. In fact, his company has never had a client fire them. Most of Computer Support Team clients have a 10-plus-year history with them.

Based on the years of experience with businesses, Scott E. realized the technology must help their client's productivity and bottom line. He helps CEO's leverage the technology available to them to increase their profit.

He states: Computer Support Team's business model puts the risk on us, not on our client.

Scott E. adds: Our mission statement explains it best. Our Mission is to gain mutual trust and respect by providing superior technology consulting and solutions that:
- *BUSINESS OWNERS value as helping their bottom line*
- *EXECUTIVES benefit from productive employees*
- *END USERS want to refer*
- *CST TEAM MEMBERS are proud of*
- *VENDORS want to recommend*

Scott E. is currently working with the world's most famous hacker to help businesses with the most destructive threat to a business, cyber security. Through education and phishing tests he is helping businesses build their human firewall. This lead to the opportunity to co-author a book on cyber-security called *Easy Prey*.

Scott E. and Computer Support Team are your Technology Consultants. They serve your business interests and make sure you are leveraging the best solution to be as productive and profitable as possible, all with a guarantee.

You can connect with Scott E. at:
- ScottE@YourCST.com
- www.YourCST.com
- www.linkedin.com/in/ScottEPalmquist

CHAPTER 21

HOW CLOUD COMPUTING IS THE ANSWER TO MOST CYBER-SECURITY CONCERNS

BY FRANK M. DeBENEDETTO

Many of us have in some way or form heard of the new technology being offered by some of the world's largest technology corporations, such as Microsoft, Amazon, and Google, but how many people actually know the technicalities and advantages of cloud computing in relation to small businesses? Many business owners aren't even certain where or what the cloud is, and, with so many options, they can become paralyzed with indecision.

WHAT DOES CLOUD COMPUTING HAVE TO DO WITH YOUR CAR?

One way to describe the shift towards cloud computing is to compare it to how you obtained your car. Let's assume that at some point in the past you went shopping for a new car. You likely looked at several models and test drove some until you made a choice based both on price and value. Once you drove that car off the lot, you assumed a certain level of responsibility to keep it performing. You had to insure it, protect it in your garage, get the oil changed, have the tires rotated and get it regularly serviced. If you were diligent, you took it in for regular maintenance and didn't just wait until you were on the side of the road with the hazards on and the tow truck en route. The money that you paid was a capital outlay and eventually you paid that car off. Years later, that car doesn't exactly perform the way it did when you first purchased it. The wear and tear from using it all these years has started to take its toll, but you justify the subpar performance because you no longer have a car payment. You know, however, that you are treading on borrowed time because eventually the cost of maintaining that old car exceeds a certain financial threshold and you repeat the same exercise and buy another vehicle.

This is exactly the same concept when you purchase and own servers and other on-premise technology. You make a capital investment in hardware that must be maintained and protected from a myriad of risks and eventually it becomes slow and outdated and must be replaced. A typical lifecycle lasts three to seven years. Many business owners choose, knowingly or unknowingly and at their own risk, to neglect those servers by not backing them up properly and not maintaining or protecting them. Many times, their intentions are good but running their business gets in the way and they aren't sure where to turn. The upside is that it costs little to nothing on a monthly basis to neglect your technology. The downside is that you leave yourself wide open to risks that could shutter your business. Imagine if your car salesman told you to just drive your new car until it broke down on the side of the road and then have it serviced? You would think he was crazy and likely buy the car somewhere else. This, however, happens every day in the world of technology.

Another interesting thing happens along the way with advances in features and functionality. When you purchased your new car, there were certain options available. You probably selected as many of those options as you could afford and then did without the others. As time goes on, however, you notice many of those items that were considered luxuries now becoming standard features on the newer models. Luxuries such as navigation, rear facing backup cameras and Bluetooth have become standard options. Technology that was once nice to have suddenly becomes a necessity that dramatically improves the efficiency and safety of our lives and may even save us money over time. Unfortunately, your car doesn't have these features because you purchased it years ago and you didn't have the extra capital to spend at the time. For now, you do without and earnestly look forward to the day when you can replace it. But that's years off and you dread having to spend more capital.

Again, this is what happens to many business owners. They purchased hardware years ago that was cutting edge but now lacks the features and benefits of modern technology. With technology changing so rapidly, it's hard not to get caught up in this trap. Destined to get their money's worth, they "drive" this hardware as long as they can. Often, they don't know what they don't know, and they simply run their business with what they have and usually at a disadvantage.

Everyone knows someone who makes the decision not to purchase a car but rather lease one. They are able to get more car and more options than they usually could if they had to purchase one because the capital requirements are lower. They usually have a new car every three years and rarely ever complain about the dreaded expenses that the owners of an old car encounter. Since they regularly lease a new car at predetermined intervals, they also always have the latest in modern safety and convenience. With maintenance usually included in the lease payment, they get the car regularly serviced and any recalls are immediately addressed. They don't need to educate themselves as a mechanic because the dealership handles everything for them. You could argue that they will always have a car payment and that they will never own the car. The leasee will tell you that they don't want to own the car and all the problems that come along with ownership as the car ages. They simply want to drive the car and enjoy the peace of mind and convenience that accompanies the latest options.

Imagine if you could apply the same logic to your technology? Instead of large capital outlays on technology every three to seven years, you could trade it for a monthly operating cost and get more features and have greater protection than you normally could afford. Imagine if you automatically had the latest technology available to you and it actually helped increase business, made you more efficient and you were in control of your monthly expense without having to really own much of anything? What if you could use pretty much any inexpensive device to access your technology and leave all the complexities, security concerns and maintenance to the professionals while you focused on running your business? Imagine no more. This is the world of cloud computing and, with the proper guidance, you can be enjoying it in your business today. In fact, it's likely that you are already using certain aspects of cloud computer even if you may not know it.

BUY SERVICES, NOT SERVERS

Now that you have a better understanding conceptually of cloud computing, we can explore the practicality of using the cloud in the workplace. The term "cloud" simply means that the majority of the expensive and complex hardware that drives the technology resides in another location such as a data center and is accessed via the Internet. These data centers are built with three main objectives: physical security, continuous power and redundant Internet connectivity. No small business could ever cost-effectively duplicate the same level of protection and continuity of service at the local level. Rather than continuing down the same path of recycling servers, you can replace them and their functionality with services that you pay for via a monthly subscription.

For many business owners, the thought of relinquishing control of their servers and putting their data somewhere in the cloud can be daunting. Valid concerns include questions over where the data actually resides or what happens to that data if the cloud vendor should go out of business. Regulatory compliance requirements from HIPAA and FINRA could also play a factor when planning a move to the cloud. Before we address these concerns, however, think about what you are doing today. Are your servers locked in a secure, climate-controlled room with audited access or are they sitting out in the open in someone's office or hallway? What happens today when the power goes out due to inclement weather or an accident? Do you have a generator in the office? What happens today if the Internet goes down? Do you have a redundant connection? Will you currently pass an audit if you are subject to regulatory compliance? In almost every instance, it becomes clear that the cloud is a much safer alternative to your current, local technology environment. The bottom line is you need to compare cloud services to what you should have in your office and not necessarily to what you do have.

Getting back to the concern over the location of your data, let's identify the three major types of cloud service providers. The first type would be those cloud services powered by global leaders in technology such as Microsoft, Google and Amazon. These companies clearly have a low risk of going out of business and they use multiple, redundant data centers around the world. The downside is that it is highly unlikely that you will know exactly where your data actually resides. In many instances, a business owner may not care but if that is too great of a concern, they may want to consider a national or regional cloud service provider such as OS33. At this level, a business owner will usually have direct knowledge over the location and name of the data center housing their data and they will know where it may be stored for redundancy in the case of disaster recovery. These national firms are usually large enough that they have been fully vetted by third party auditors and will have passed many of the requirements of regulatory compliance. The last type of cloud service provider can be found at the local level and usually involves a smaller IT firm who has crafted their own solution in their own or a locally outsourced data center. While these cloud services may be cost effective, you must be certain that the provider won't go out of business and that they have the proper security controls in place. Despite any concerns, in reality, your overall technology platform will come from a variety and not just one cloud service provider.

Consider this fact: when you trade your servers for services, you automatically get enterprise class technology. You no longer have the ability to turn a blind eye and save a few dollars. You can't ask the cloud service provider to put you in a less secure data center, skip a few backups each week and not use antivirus. No matter which provider you use, as soon as you switch to the cloud, you immediately increase security and improve business continuity.

CYBER SECURITY CONCERNS

Cyber security is critical because everyone and everything is after your most valuable asset – your data. An entire underground economy exists solely to steal your sensitive data and then trade it on the black market for financial gain. Cyber security risks include some of the following:
- Physical security
- Malware such as viruses, ransomware, worms and Trojan horses
- Loss of data on smartphones and tablets or laptops
- Exploits in unpatched operating systems or software
- SPAM
- Rogue employees
- Lack of two factor authentication
- Remote Accessibility
- Intrusion Attempts

In order to fully understand how cloud computing can mitigate most of these cyber security risks, it's important to take stock of what a business that has moved to the cloud actually looks like. We already know that the servers are usually eliminated from the office. In doing so, we jettison that capital expense while drastically improving physical security. If the servers are gone, we no longer have the burden of preventing the server from being stolen. We don't have to worry about backups, antivirus, patching or protection from outside intrusions, and we don't have to worry about power or Internet connectivity bringing a business to a halt. Business continuity is nearly guaranteed. Many of the concerns that burdened that business owner are now the responsibility of the cloud service provider.

If the goal of nearly all cyber security attacks is to gain access to your data and that data has been removed from your office, the local infrastructure is greatly simplified. With many cloud services, the application and the data are both located in the data center. That means the data may never leave the data center. Only keyboard clicks, mouse movements and video traverses the Internet. In other instances, data travels across a secure tunnel called a virtual private network (VPN). Either way, security is improved and risk is reduced.

Remote access to your data by authorized individuals is equally as important. All cloud services have granular control and allow you to audit who accesses the data. While most security focuses on outside threats, one of the most overlooked risks is in the form of an internal employee who has already been granted access. This audit trail helps you keep track and contain any damage before it gets too out of hand. Hosted email is probably one of the most popular and widely-used cloud services. Many services include robust SPAM and virus filters that block threats before they ever reach your email client. Two-factor authentication is another easily implemented feature of most cloud platforms. This combines something you know (password) with something you have (Smartphone with a texted PIN). That way, no one can gain access with just your password. This second method of authentication greatly increases security. Most cloud service providers have apps that reside on your Smartphone and can be used to access data and email. In the event that the device is lost or stolen, the Smartphone can be locked or remotely wiped to prevent data loss.

The bottom line is that cloud computing is the direction that all technology is headed. Think of a world where all you can do is lease a high end automobile and that should give you a pretty good idea of the future of technology. No matter which cloud service providers you choose, you are guaranteed to have greater security than what you have today.

About Frank

Frank M. DeBenedetto has spent the past two decades passionately helping business owners navigate the complex world of technology. His interest in technology began back in college when he had trouble finding someone to fix the computer he was using to write lab reports. After watching one of his classmates reinstall the operating system, he became enamored with computers and their impact on our lives. Frank has always been determined to keep pace with modern technology and, today, that path has led him to become a highly sought-after expert in the area of cloud computing.

A graduate of Rutgers University, Frank holds a Bachelor of Science degree in Mechanical Engineering. While pondering graduate school, Frank began his career in the financial services industry with The Guardian. He became life and health insurance licensed and passed the Series 7, 63 and 24 securities licensing exams. Before finally shifting his educational focus towards technology, he earned two designations from the American College of Financial Services – Chartered Life Underwriter (CLU) and Chartered Financial Consultant (ChFC). After a period of selling, Frank found his niche in helping other financial services professionals utilize technology to grow their businesses. Soon after, his entrepreneurial spirit took over and he left the industry to fully concentrate his efforts on building a technology consulting firm.

Frank M. DeBenedetto is the President and Chief Technology Advisor of Two River Technology Group, a technology solutions provider located in Shrewsbury, NJ. After many years of honing his technical skills in the enterprise, he brought his style of consulting to the small-to-midsize business marketplace. With an emphasis on managed services, managed security and hosted voice over IP (VoIP), Frank has helped grow TRTG into one of the premier cloud service providers in the area. Today, he spends the majority of his professional time on new business development.

Frank has been quoted in many publications and is a regular contributor to several blogs, podcasts and newspapers. He frequently speaks at seminars and webinars on current trends in technology and he's the author of a book that offers practical advice on technology to the small business owner.

Frank enjoys spending quality time away from technology with his family and close group of friends. He is an avid Rutgers football fan and can be frequently found in Madison Square Garden at a New York Rangers hockey game. In his spare time, Frank enjoys reading Stephen King, playing the guitar, golfing and skiing. Frank currently resides in Middletown, NJ with his daughter, Evangeline.

You can connect with Frank at:
- fmdb@tworivertech.com
- https://twitter.com/frankienextdoor
- https://www.linkedin.com/in/frankdebenedetto

CHAPTER 22

WHAT TO DO IF YOU'VE BEEN HACKED

BY GREG BLANC

Jim arrived at 8:00 a.m. like he did every day, brewed his Keurig pod and sat down to log into his system. When he tried to log in, he was booted a number of times, for failed password. He noticed others around him the office having the same issue, and then the call came "Jim, we have a problem, our website has been blocked, no one can log in, something about denial of service or something like that."

Jim began began to panic, and then the other shoe fell. "Yes Mr. Mars, this is Sally at your bank. It seems you are overdrawn on your account." How could that be, Jim had just logged into his bank account yesterday online, and there was over $5000 in checking alone.

"There must be a mistake, shouldn't the overdraft funds in my savings cover everything?"

"Mr. Mars, that is the problem, there is nothing in your Savings account. It seems you transferred all of the funds from your accounts yesterday to another bank in the Caymans."

Jim almost dropped the phone… and he heard a voice from across the office, "Hey guys! I think we have been hacked!"

If you haven't been hacked already in some way, consider yourself in an ever-diminishing category.

The year's digital security outlook doesn't exactly inspire hope: The survey found that 52% of respondents believe they'll "likely" be hit by a successful cyber-attack this year, up from 39% last year. And even more respondents, 71% of them, admit that they fell victim to a successful cyber-attack in the prior year.
~ According to Robert Hackett of Time Inc. Network.

Most of us have experienced some form of Cyber-crime, it ranges from petty theft of your ID and or credit cards, intrusion of unauthorized withdrawals from your bank account all the way up to the constant onslaught of possible fraud by unscrupulous thieves. The greatest threats are hiding out on the dark web, (parts of the World Wide Web that fly under the radar because they exist in an unindexed format, and therefore are not recognized by browsers in typical searches), and they want to hack into your business or medical practices, steal your confidential data and compromise your clients.

If you haven't had to deal with Cybercrime, then read on, and if you have, then you have even more to gain by continuing to read on.

In the scenario described above, we would ask Jim and his colleagues a few questions to ascertain the nature of the breach. There are indicators that suggest you have been hacked, here are just a few examples:

- Frequent Random Pop-ups. You will notice that all of a sudden you are plagued with pop-ups when you are on-line. You can tell if you notice this more prominently on sites you are familiar with. When getting random pop-ups, check other networks to see if they come up there as well, if not, there is a good chance you have been hacked.
- Unwanted browser toolbars with names that seem to indicate the toolbar is supposed to help you. Unless you recognize the toolbar as coming from a very well-known source, it is not to be trusted.
- Re-direction of Internet searches. Hackers are paid to redirect your searches to locations other than what you wanted.
- Fake anti-virus messages, in slight decline these days, but none-the-less formidable. If you do not recognize the name of the program, do not engage.
- Your friends report receiving fake emails from your email account.
- Your on-line password suddenly changes.

- Unexpected Software appears on your system.
- The remote mouse control moves on its own, where the cursor is moving without your help.
- Your Anti-virus program is disabled.
- You are missing money from your accounts or charges are duplicated.
- You get calls from vendors regarding non-payment of shipped goods.

YOU'RE NOT THE FIRST, AND WON'T BE THE LAST

It may or may not be comforting, but you must consider the common assumption in the industry these days is that there are only two kinds of companies, the ones that have been hacked and the ones who don't yet know they've been hacked. It is recommended that you will want to run through a series of actions to minimize the exposure, downtime, and repair any damage done. We would begin by backing up your critical data to a secure location. The on-line interaction that led to the breach can often be remedied by resetting the browser.

Next, you'll want to reset your passwords. If you have already been locked out, you will need to go through the reset and make sure to use high level passwords that are alphanumeric and contain special characters. Try not to reuse the passwords you have used in the past. Password Manager, (a free application that allows you to safely store all of your passwords in a secure password vault), is a great option if keeping up with passwords is a concern for you. Hackers will use the information they obtain to try to access other accounts.

WITH PAIN COMES WISDOM

The next thing to get to is a full scan of your system by using the anti-virus program that you have. It is possible that you have not been keeping up with the notices to update the program. It is often true, that we ignore those reminders and end up wishing we had not. The best way to run the scan is to shut down your computer and restart in safe mode, after which you will want to run a virus scan. Be sure to check for spyware, malware, and any other viruses that may still be lingering on your network, and capturing your keystrokes.

[Note: IF you find malware after the scan, you will want to reset the passwords again, after a re-boot of the system.]

Verify details of your account records, shipping addresses and processing account records, and examine any newly installed applications that may have been the Trojan, or malware that is hidden in code that you download, unaware of their presence. Once activated the Trojan virus can enable cybercriminals to spy on you, steal your sensitive data, and gain access to other files on your system.

Make certain to secure all other devices on the network and ask any other users to reset their browsers, and passwords, we would then go through a thorough scan of the entire system.

Instigate an incident report and broadcast that goes out to all concerned parties. Inform your financial institutions, they will have advice on what to do to further protect your funds.

MITIGATION

Minimize the damage, and protect your assets by placing an alert on your credit through the credit agencies (Equifax, Experian, and TransUnion) and request a 90-day credit alert. These reporting agencies are responsible for contacting the other institutions in this industry for unified accuracy. This alert tells businesses to contact you before opening any new accounts in your name, or company name. You can renew the alert after 90 days if you feel it is warranted.

As you have heard on almost daily basis, sophisticated clients have been susceptible to data breach due to theft or even their own negligence. An example in recent news is of Wells Fargo & Co. being investigated by the Connecticut attorney general for potentially disclosing customers' Social Security numbers as part of a fraud investigation when it forwarded subpoenas to customers that contained the confidential information of more than 9 million individuals.

In the case of a data breach, the cover-up can be worse than the crime. Forty-six states require some form of notification for data breach as well as various Federal laws. The typical state statute, the duty to notify applies whenever there has been an unauthorized access of a system where digital data is acquired; the security or confidentiality of personal information is compromised; the breach involves a database of personal information about more than one individual and the breach causes or has the potential of causing loss, injury or harm to an individual.

It is sometimes difficult to identify what exactly was taken. This is the reason a complete investigation must be conducted. This can prove very costly. It is understandable that a company will not want to suffer the public relations hit of admitting to a data breach, but it can be far worse financially to hold off notifying the potentially-harmed parties when a company has a reasonable belief of a breach. A more advisable approach is to notify all potential victims of the possibility of a breach while you are in the process of conducting the investigation. In this way you have communicated the threat and given all concerned parties the greatest possible edge at preventing further damage. In the case of a false alarm, clients will still realize that you had their best interest at heart.

BUTTON DOWN THE DETAILS

A proper investigation will include understanding not just how, but when the breach occurred and be able to determine the extent of the exposure/ loss. Any claims by clients should be explored with great attention to detail. Failure to do so can result in fines due to non-compliance of statutes, and further expose your company to loss of revenue.

Notifying potential victims includes offering them information and resources that are necessary for them to protect themselves moving forward. Doing this effectively will remedy some of the hardship implicated by the breach itself, especially these days when most people are aware of the nefarious nature of today's digital world.

To protect yourself even further, if you are a company that maintains a database with personal and protected information, especially Physicians and Lawyers, you will want to invest in insurance to cover losses that stem from data breach. Several insurance providers exist, but several have shortcomings in their coverages, so be sure to sit down with your representatives and follow the protocols that they have outlined for you.

SEVEN SIMPLE STEPS TO SECURE YOUR COMPUTER FROM MALICIOUS ATTACKS AND AVOID EXPENSIVE REPAIR BILLS

1.) Keep an up-to-date a are running on your system at all times. I recommend [AVG anti-virus] for two simple reasons:
   (a) It detects and removes spyware and malware programs that a lot of the more well-known (and more expensive) anti-virus software programs miss.
   (b) It does it for about half the price.

It also has an auto scan and update feature that will make sure your computer is running the most current protection available and regularly scanning for threats.

2.) Start using an alternative web browser to Internet Explorer such as Mozilla Firefox. Just recently, hackers have figured out a way to access and download malicious programs to your computer via a security hole in IE. What is amazing about this is that you don't even have to click on anything or download a program to get infected. You are especially vulnerable if you have an older version of Windows such as Windows 98.

Mozilla is a completely free web browser that does not have the same security problems as IE. Many of my clients even report back that they like their Mozilla browser better than Internet Explorer. Switching from IE to Mozilla is a simple and cost-free way to add another layer of security to your computer.

3.) Use an alternative e-mail program other than Outlook Express. Outlook Express is notorious for security holes. If you don't have the latest security updates, hackers can send you e-mails with viruses that automatically open and install themselves without you even opening or previewing the e-mail and its attachments. I recommend that you either upgrade Outlook Express to a newer, more secure version of Outlook or switch to Mozilla's Thunderbird E-mail software.

4.) Never open suspicious looking e-mails or attachments. This goes without saying because most viruses are replicated via e-mail. If it looks suspicious, delete it immediately!

5.) Stop using peer-to-peer file sharing sites and downloading "cute" programs. Think of it like cyber candy. Hackers use these cute and funny programs as bait to get you to download their destructive programs. These are guaranteed ways of contracting malicious viruses, spyware, and malware. Also, peer-to-peer file sharing sites like KaZaa are mine fields of malicious programs. NEVER access those sites or download the programs that run them.

6.) Set up a firewall. A firewall is simply a device that acts as a buffer between you and the big, wild world of the Internet. Many users will get a DSL or cable Internet connection and plug it directly into their computer with no firewall in between.

The one thing you have to remember about the Internet is that it is a big open field. You have access to the world, but on the flip side, the world has access to YOU. Hackers have programs that automatically scan the Internet for computers connected via a cable or DSL connection without a firewall. Once they find one, they access your computer, download vicious programs, and can even use YOUR computer to send viruses to your friends and other computers, all without your knowledge or consent.

No one really thinks about losing all of the data on their computer or having it compromised until it actually happens. By then, it is either too late and you have lost EVERYTHING or it will take a lot of money paid to a specialist to recover your files.

7.) I cannot stress the importance of backing up your files enough. If the files on your computer are important to you, then it is about time you got serious about protecting them by backing up every night.

FBI PROCEDURES

Document to the Proper Authorities – Today's world is more interconnected than ever before. Yet, for all its advantages, increased connectivity brings increased risk of theft, fraud, and abuse. Complementary cybersecurity and law enforcement capabilities are critical to safeguarding and securing cyberspace. Law enforcement performs an essential role in achieving our nation's cybersecurity objectives by investigating a wide range of cybercrimes, from theft and fraud to child exploitation, and apprehending and prosecuting those responsible. The Department of Homeland Security (DHS) works with other federal agencies to conduct high-impact criminal investigations to disrupt and defeat cyber criminals, prioritize the recruitment and training of technical experts, develop standardized methods, and broadly share cyber response best practices and tools. Criminal investigators and network security experts with deep understanding of the technologies malicious actors are using and the specific vulnerabilities they are targeting, work to effectively respond to and investigate cyber incidents.

DHS components such as the U.S. Secret Service and U.S. Immigration and Customs Enforcement (ICE) have special divisions dedicated to combating cybercrime. Be sure to contact Law Enforcement Cyber Incident Reporting. This resource provides for state, and local enforcement on when, what and how to report a cyber-incident to a federal entity.

About Greg

Working within the same organization for over thirty years, there have been many challenges, as well as many successes. This wealth of this experience provided Greg Blanc with the opportunity to share and contribute what he knows with others. Since his early beginnings, Greg has dedicated himself to a consistent standard of excellence, creating a natural progression to where he is now.

As the CEO of EvolvTec, he continues to work with many of the same people that formed a team with the same high standards. Greg believes in one fundamental discipline that has made the difference for EvolvTec: always giving the customer what they want. He feels strongly about the importance of listening to what prospective clients are challenged with and working with them to develop a solution that will exceed their expectations. Greg combines their needs and the expertise of his team of engineers to provide the perfect solution. Here's how:

- --Conduct surveys, listen to what clients have to say
- --Over communicate – don't wait until a customer asks for an update
- --Treat customers like family
- --Treat Employees like they are customers
- --Be proactive, anticipate possible problems and have solutions ready
- --Provide well trained professionals to make it right
- --Always be professional, kind and courteous
- --Be highly available – 24X7, 365 days of the year
- --Provide a positive customer experience that people will remember and talk about
- --Always treat customers as if they will refer you to others, because they will

Greg understands listening to people and working hard is the path to success. People recognize the focus and dedication that he brings and appreciate his expectation to provide quality work and experience for customers and fellow associates. Over the years, he has been involved in almost every department in the company, and has come to realize how critical and challenging quality is to running a successful company. This realization, along with the experience he brings, has inspired him to build a high level of standards in all aspects of the company.

Greg shares his foundation and vision to consistently grow the service offering and, in a relatively short period of time, EvolvTec has opened eight locations including; Tallahassee, Tampa, Jacksonville, Orlando, Ocala, Pensacola, and then Fort Myers. This complements well with the headquarters located in Fort Lauderdale, becoming one of only a few companies having the footprint to cover the entire state and making them the natural choice for many State Agencies. They have worked with most agencies within the state, including: Department of Labor, Highway Safety, Transportation, Business and Professional Regulations, Florida Highway Patrol and more.

As CEO, Greg Blanc empowers his team and calls on them to bring not just their technical skill, but their ability to satisfy the customer's needs. He prefers to call the field service engineers, Customer Engineers (CE) because they don't just fix machines; they help customers with what they need so they can perform their duties. All of the CEs are continuing to learn current and emerging technologies so they can evolve and bring those technologies to benefit clients.

CHAPTER 23

SPAM

BY CRAIG RAY

It has been 38 years since the invention of email, and today, it is still the number one communication tool. However, it also contributed to a new scheme of electronic criminal activity known as SPAM. Unfortunately, email is one of the most widely-used approaches for cybercrimes. Most Americans know of and have dealt with spam in some way or form. . . No, not the less than appetizing canned meat product. Spam is defined as either malicious or irrelevant messages sent to a large number of people, which may include emails, text messages, instant messages, phone calls or voicemails, and even paper mail. Currently, a breathtaking nine out of ten emails that are sent globally are considered to be spam; thus, the average American spends around twenty minutes every day dealing with and deleting spam in various forms. Not only is spam irritating and time-consuming, but it may be a form of cybercrime or scams.

THE HISTORY OF SPAM

Though spam has existed since near the invention of paper mail in forms of propaganda and scams, notably the spamming telegram given by the Bank Western Union, for the purpose of this chapter we will focus on electronic spam specifically. Though it has been around for quite a while, the origin of the term spam is very modern. Many of us are familiar with the famous British comedy television series, "Monty Python" – this is where the now dictionary-recognized term spam originated. The now-hysterical scene in which a group of Vikings begins yelling the word "spam" louder and louder was thought to represent the increasing volume of irrelevant or malicious messages being sent and received online. This translated to harmless pranks played by users of multi-player network dungeon games during the late eighties, in which the inbox of a victim would be filled with irrelevant messages.

Though spam did not become a widely-known term until the invention of email in the early 2000's, the first piece of spam was sent electronically as early as 1978. During 1994, with the first users of email and the widespread use of the Internet, spam became a means of business practice. From this time until the present, the usage of spam has increased phenomenally, making it one of the biggest illegal businesses to take place in modern First World Countries.

In 2003, the first bill passed by Congress with the intentions of eradicating spam emails was put into action, cleverly titled "The Can-Spam Act." As a result, during the year 2004, spam arrests took off like never before seen, including the apprehension of a New Yorker named Howard Carmak, following the over 800 million emails he sent from stolen identities. Another notorious spammer, Vardan Kushner, was found dead in his apartment in 2005, following the emailing of spam to what was believed to be every single one of Russia's computer user's. His death is considered to be murder, as the spammer was found to have passed due to blunt force trauma to the head. To this day, the murder case remains cold, and it is speculated as to whether or not the murder was inspired by his spamming.

The following year an even more disturbing occurrence happened to a large-scale spammer. When Davis Wolfgang Hawk went into hiding after he was discovered as a high-profile cybercriminal, the graves of his parents were strangely given to the greatest digital media and technology company at that time, AOL. AOL claimed their intentions were to dig up and keep any gold and silver that was thought to be buried among Hawk's parents, to keep as compensation for the money lost to Hawk. In 2008, "Spam King" Eddie Davidson was also involved in a rather unpleasant crime, killing both his child and wife after escaping from the prison camp in which he was being detained at the time. Following the murder of his family, Davidson also killed himself.

TYPES OF SPAM AND HOW THEY WORK

Do you ever remember getting a message from a friend claiming you must send it on to many others or else something terrible will occur to you? This may have 'scared the daylights out of you' as a child or teenager. "Chainmail" is a type of spam in which receivers are told to forward the message though it is generally irrelevant. The term for email spam is unsolicited commercial email.

Though far less commonplace than emailing spam, instant messaging spam is also very prevalent, especially on servers such as AIM and Omegle, as opposed to on social network instant messaging systems.

Social networking spam is the third most common spam, including malicious links and chain comments. Many spam programs are spread through links claiming to be shocking and interesting information, such as Robin William's suicide video or an inappropriate video of yourself. When the link is opened, it often directs you to another web page asking for shares and access to your Facebook account, once given access the program may send friends spam or repost the link without your permission. This may seem harmless enough at face value, but often these links also contain malware in which your personal information may be stolen, or viruses may be downloaded onto your device. Chain comments are very similar to chain emails, except they are spread through reposting a comment instead of forwarding an email.

"Social spam" is a bit of a difficult subject to understand. It is defined as the submission of hate, threats, violence, profanity, insults, or anything else considered to be socially unacceptable online behavior. This form of online harassment can occur not only on social networks but any website where a person may add any type of propaganda. Some other names for this type of spam or online behavior include "trolling" or "cyberbullying." Though it may be hard to find the guilty party and the online platform used, especially when many social media sites have little or no rules, these kinds of harassing messages often carry some sort of criminal charges with varying degrees of severity by the state.

Online video games also include instant messaging to allow different players to communicate with each other. This type of gaming communication enables the game playing experience to be rich, but, as with every social outlet on the Internet, gaming comes with its own set of spam. In fact, as previously mentioned, some of the original spam happened through online gaming. The qualifications for spam are different in every video game or with every developer; however, it often includes repeatedly sending messages, sending harassing messages, asking players for real money in return for something digital that would benefit them in the game, or repeatedly using the same "attack" to win a level.

"Spamdexing" is a term that includes spam-favoring search engines, usually with a small amount of traffic; however, because of the increased popularity of only using certain, trusted search engines, such as Bing, Yahoo or Google as opposed to at the beginning of the Internet, where search engines were not as well known or used as they are today, this type of spam is becoming less and less popular.

The most common type of spam is advertising spam, this is usually used to promote either legitimate or illegitimate businesses or goods, and may range from dating websites to antivirus programs to even presidential candidates. With this kind of spam, the only threat it poses is possibly slowing down your computer's speed and the time it takes to load your emails, but it is a nuisance nonetheless, and may cost a victim a great deal of time in going through and deleting these kinds of spam.

Another very common type of spam that many of us have had to deal with is spam generated by malware, particularly by viruses. Once infected, your computer may display pop-ups, and the amount of spam in your inboxes will increase drastically. Virus and spam creators have teamed up to create this kind of malware, with the result benefiting both, either by being paid by spammers or being able to crash computers through spam on the virus creator's side and by being able to quickly send large amounts of spam with little effort by spammers. Because it is sent from a virus instead of from another type of computer system that may be trackable by authorities through an I.P. address, these types of spam are favored by many cybercriminals. This type of spam commonly includes fake emails or links to websites that are made to appear to be sent from a legitimate source. Once opened, these links or downloads may include all different sorts of malware, from downloads that may steal your information to ransomware.

An increasing and dangerous version of spam is phishing. Phishing is where criminals attempt to steal data such as bank information or social security number by pretending to be a legitimate source, sometimes claiming that a bank account has been frozen, or the victim's identity has been stolen. Unlike other types of spam, phishing may be extremely hard to identify, as counterfeiting bank logo's and login systems have become a prevalent crime on the black market. This type of spam is becoming so out of control that over eighty percent of American businesses reported having phishing attacks within the last year, along with the fifty-eight percent of businesses who are reported believing that phishing is increasing as a means of spam.

HOW TO PROTECT YOURSELF AGAINST SPAM

An excellent way to steer clear of spam is keeping track of what websites you subscribe to, and whether they are legitimate enough not to send spam. For example, it may not be in your best interest to subscribe to a small, for prophet, gaming website. If you do subscribe to various websites, it is suggested that you create an email for spam and recreational usage, and another for business and social communication, so spam does not get in the way of your daily life.

In addition to this, disable automatic downloads, don't go to secure websites, and never download anything unless doing a scan and research to know the download will be malware free. Taking this step will help in keeping malware, such as viruses which produce scams, from your computer. In addition to this, make sure that you have security programs such as firewalls and antivirus downloaded, as well as checking to make sure your subscription to the company, if applicable, is still good, and that your security programs are up to date.

To avoid malware, ensuring that your computer is up-to-date is also an important aspect of security, with every new operating system developer improving firewalls and make it more complicated for malware to get through. Though this may seem to be impractical and expensive, many times you do not need to replace a whole device, but instead download the new operating system on an older computer that it is compatible with, which is usually offered at a reasonable price.

A less obvious way of making sure that spam and viruses do not get through is checking to make sure Internet connections are safe when using a device at a location other than in your home. In most office environments, Internet connections are very secure. However, other public locations, such as airports, coffee shops, and hotels might include insecure networks, often from other customer's devices. Many legitimate public networks will require a user to agree to an acceptable usage contract, which prohibits other users from infecting different computers on the public network.

Phishing sites and emails are sometimes very difficult to avoid. However, you can do some extra things to ensure your safety. Foremost, never give your bank information over email without first contacting them to ensure it is legitimate, often banks will contact you through phone calls as well as emails or text messages, this is a good indication that the email is not from a phishing source. You can also do research on phishing to determine whether a website or email is legitimate on an individual basis. Phishing programs are not generally diverse; therefore, chances are others online have been fooled by any phishing program trying to contact you.

Though spam seems to be not only here to stay but increasing, there are a number of things you can do to protect yourself and your loved one's from attacks as we have discussed.

About Craig

Craig Ray, Owner and Chief Technology Advisor of Legal Works, loves helping people and their businesses achieve their goals by setting up efficient networks. This work is very meaningful to Craig as it allows him to do what he does best while helping business do what they do best. After many years of experience and honing his technical skills in Information Technology, Craig has brought WORRY-FREE IT to many types of business. Craig is especially passionate about helping law firms focus on the LAW, not IT.

Craig and his company are truly passionate about building an IT business that delivers uncommon service to his customers — WORRY-FREE IT. He not only solves problems, but he will also design solutions. When you have technology needs, Craig and his company are your one-stop shop. Craig wants to help Law Firms see the true competitive advantages technology can deliver, and not view it as an expensive non-billable need and source of problems. Craig and Legal Works will arm you with a WORRY-FREE IT adviser who can help your business tame technology and turn it into a powerful, competitive weapon instead of an enormous financial strain and source of problems!

Craig earned his Bachelors of Science in Business at the University of California, Los Angeles. He also earned a CIS degree from DeVry University where he specialized in Information Systems Security and Computer Forensics. He has also earned many specialized certifications, including Cisco Certified Internetwork Expert - Security (CCIE Security), Certified HIPPA Professional (CHSP), and from Microsoft. In 1992, Craig opened his own successful IT company, ProTech Networks.

Craig also loves helping the community. Since 2006, Craig has been a member of the Rotary International, and he served as the President of the Harrison County, WV Rotary Club from 2013-2014. In 2015, Craig earned a Service and Dedication Award from the Rotary Club of Harrison County due to his longs hours and dedication to the community.

You can connect with Craig Ray at: craig@legal.works

CHAPTER 24

LOCKING THE DOOR

BY ALAN ADCOCK

In the late 1990's I needed to transfer some files from my work computer to my home PC. I opened a few ports, started up the FTP software and went to the office. Transferring the files was no problem, but when I arrived home several hours later I noticed a lot of drive activity. Turned out someone had discovered the FTP site I left open and was using it to distribute their counterfeit software. It only took a few hours for someone on the Internet to find the site I left open.

This occurred in the early days of the Internet. Today, the number of IP connected devices has increased rapidly and the number of probing attacks on IPs has increased even faster. As The Gartner Group points out, "All organizations should now assume they are in a state of continuous compromise."

A prospective medical practice client recently called my company for help. They had a similar firewall port issue. One of their IT staff had left some ports open and as a result a hacker leaked confidential patient information onto the Internet. This resulted in a Health and Human Services, Office for Civil Rights investigation—and required a breach notification be sent from the medical practice to all of its patients. Ouch!

YOUR FIRST LINE OF DEFENSE

Today's businesses rely heavily on Internet connectivity for email, web, and remote access to office information from mobile devices, laptops, and PCs. Unfortunately, with the convenience of connectivity comes great risk of unauthorized users gaining access to your business data for theft, harm, or destruction. The speed at which an unprotected network or mobile computer can be compromised is staggering. Simply put, your business has no business connecting to the Internet without serious protection. With the "business network" now extending to mobile devices, home offices, and the "cloud," securing the perimeter is no longer restricted to the brick and mortar office.

Here are a few questions to consider:

1. How do you defend your business data from nefarious outsiders while allowing workers remote access to resources?
2. How do you guard against sensitive information, like Social Security or credit card numbers, leaking out of your network and leaving you, as the business owner, open to huge fines and possible prosecution?
3. How do you guard against employees using the Internet in inappropriate or illegal ways?
4. How do you protect your business from malicious software designed to either steal or destroy your corporate data?

The answer is...a modern business firewall, which addresses these and many other issues. A firewall is designed to keep out the traffic you don't want, while allowing the traffic you do want in. This is why IT professionals say **a hardware firewall is the first line of defense for the modern office.**

FIREWALLS 101

Before we continue, let's cover some basics. There are two types of firewalls: software and hardware.

A "software firewall" is an application installed on a single computer, often called a "personal firewall." Microsoft includes Windows Firewall in its popular desktop operating systems. While providing rudimentary protection, this software is often considered a nuisance and frequently disabled by users. Doing so leaves the user's laptop extremely vulnerable to compromise and infection, especially when connected to a public Wi-Fi hotspot. Software firewalls are also often bundled with anti-virus/

anti-malware software. The bottom line is software firewalls are chiefly for personal protection of a single device.

A "hardware firewall" is a dedicated device specifically designed for protecting a local network, such as your office PCs, servers, and printers from Internet threats. Hardware firewalls range from very simple, inexpensive, consumer-grade devices to complex machines that rapidly analyze information streaming to and from the networks of very large organizations. Fortunately, small and medium organizations are able to select from a variety of robust business-grade devices to protect their valuable data.

FIVE DANGEROUS MYTHS AND ASSUMPTIONS

Over the years, I have met with hundreds of business owners who believed—with good reason—that their networks were sufficiently protected. Here are a few of the unfortunately inaccurate statements and assumptions I've heard:

1. **"I already have a firewall from my Internet Service Provider."**
   Cable modems are not firewalls. Neither are DSL (or fiber, or T-1, etc.) converter boxes. While these boxes allow one or more computers to connect to the Internet, they provide little to no security for your network. They may "translate" your internal network addresses to a single "external" address to traverse the Internet, but a savvy hacker can easily retrace the steps back to your PC, like a burglar following his next victim home from the mall.

2. **"I've had a firewall for years."**
   Internet threats rapidly evolve. For instance, it used to be common practice for anti-virus software vendors to send out weekly updates. Today, "zero day exploits" make it necessary for anti-virus software to update several times daily. In the same manner, today's typical hacker isn't a maladjusted, geeky teenager looking for a thrill. Cybercrime is BIG business and is backed by organized crime and even nation-states. No one connected to the Internet is safe from these predators.

3. **"I am a small business. I don't have any information that anyone would want."**
Wrong! Small businesses are even more likely to be attacked than the big guys. Why? Simply put, small businesses are easier prey. Security reports, such as those from Verizon and Symantec, show attacks on small businesses are increasing annually with thieves targeting data such as credit card numbers, customer information, and even locking up computers until a "ransom" is paid.

4. **"I already bought what I need from the office supply store."**
Cheap, consumer grade broadband routers are not an option for anyone serious about their business. Low-cost routers lack the features necessary for strong perimeter defense, have minimal ability to be customized for specific business needs, provide little useful logging, and are unable to alert you of suspicious activity on your network.

5. **"So what if I get hacked? I have insurance that will cover it."**
While cyber insurance is important, there's no way to insure against a damaged reputation once news of a data breach gets out, especially if it includes customers' personal or financial information. Few businesses recover from such a blow. If the hacker obtains bank account numbers and credentials, a business can be financially wiped out overnight. Even if insurance covers the loss, the ability to pay suppliers, meet payroll, or pay taxes may not occur quickly enough to avert disaster. Consider two things: How dependent is your business on the Internet for email, ordering, etc.? How long could your business survive if a cyber-attack closed you down for three days, a week, or longer? (Hint: most businesses don't survive.)

ACRONYMS AND DEFINITIONS TO HELP YOU WADE THROUGH THE MARKETING

It seems like all IT systems get buried in a sea of acronyms that mean different things to different vendors. To help you wade through the techno-speak and marketing hype as you try to find the right firewall solution to protect your business, here are some common terms and acronyms:

DMZ: Demilitarized Zone. In firewall terms, this is a network sectioned off from the main company network, usually containing Internet-facing servers, such as web servers. Security is handled differently for these servers than for the rest of the network.

DoS: Denial of Service, a type of attack used to overload a company's computer system.

IPS: Intrusion Prevention System, a key feature of NGFW (Next Generation Firewall) that evaluates traffic coming from the Internet and compares it to signatures, much like anti-virus software does for files on a PC.

NAT: Network Address Translation is a system which allows a company's internal IP address range to communicate out to the Internet IP range. A small company will typically have 5 to 14 public IP addresses assigned by their Internet Service Provider (ISP) and have 254 internal IP addresses for servers and desktops inside the company.

NGFW – Next Generation Firewall. (All vendors want their product to be the latest and greatest!) This term is used by many vendors and refers to the same feature set as a UTM (Unified Threat Management) appliance.

Port: A number from 1 to 65535 that serves as a specific "doorway" data uses to enter or leave a network. Some ports are assigned to a particular service (email commonly uses ports 25 or 110). Opening or blocking ports is an essential part of firewall security.

SMTP / POP: Two types of email systems.

TCP, UDP: Two ways information is "packaged" for transmission across networks.

VPN: Virtual Private Network, used to create a secure "tunnel" through the Internet for business communication.

WPA2 - A recommended type of security used in Wireless networking.

UTM - Unified Threat Management, a modern, advanced firewall. Exactly the same as NGFW.

BEYOND THE BASICS

We once visited a prospective client who, when asked about their firewall, pointed to "that small box with blinking lights" on a shelf. It was a router. I don't know if their former IT vendor called it a firewall, but the client certainly felt they were protected from the Internet by those blinking lights. We had to gently break the truth that their "firewall" was no better than a butler letting in anyone who came knocking at the door. (If you're not sure you have a firewall in place today, put down this book and talk to your IT staff/vendor immediately!)

Basic firewall technology has become a key part of many companies' security defense strategy. A traditional firewall will provide packet filtering, network-and-port-address Translation (NAT), thorough inspection of Internet traffic, and virtual private network (VPN) support.

Unfortunately, cyber-attacks have become more sophisticated and are targeting more than just "big business" these days. As a result, most small and medium-sized businesses are in need of more than just a basic firewall to protect their critical data and operations. As the pace of technological change continues to move quickly, firewall technology has become much more sophisticated. These newer, more advanced firewall solutions are known as **"NextGen Firewalls"** (NGFW).

NextGen Firewalls include the typical functions of traditional firewalls, but go deeper into the layers of Internet traffic to improve filtering of network traffic dependent on the packet contents. The key differentiators between traditional and next generation firewalls include:

Anti-virus / Anti-spyware: Protects against the latest content-level threats by detecting and removing malicious software.

Anti-spam: Significantly reduces spam volume at the perimeter for superior control of email attacks and infections. The firewall manufacturer develops and maintains accurate lists of spammers and spam content.

Application Control: By using "digital fingerprints" the NGFW can identify applications even if they are not running on their traditional port numbers. Once applications are identified, policies can be added to the firewall to control access to those applications in line with corporate policies.

External Data Inclusion: For a NGFW to function properly it needs to pull data from external systems. User information from Windows Active Directory, white/black lists for IP addresses and mail servers, and web filter categorization lists are examples of external data sources firewalls need to query in order to build successful security policies.

Intrusion Prevention Service: This integrated system protects against known and unknown network-level threats, including command and control traffic and botnet attacks, by examining network traffic for attack signatures.

Reporting: NGFW should be able to create reports based on included features to provide better visibility on firewall activity.

SSL Decryption: SSL refers to a type of encrypted traffic on the Internet. It is important for a NGFW to be able to look inside this SSL traffic to make sure it is not used to circumvent other firewall controls.

User Identification and User Based Policy: In networking systems it is difficult to identify individual users, so it is important to set policies in the firewall for users to move around the network and use different PCs and laptops.

FIVE (5) BEST PRACTICES OF FIREWALL OPERATION

In my experience, sometimes even with a NGFW firewall present, the business is not truly protected. In order for a firewall to properly protect your business, you must do the following:

1. Enable the Advanced Features

While it may seem obvious to fully utilize all the features that come with a firewall, all too often firewalls are installed with only a basic setup, not utilizing the feature set originally purchased. NGFW devices have a ton of options. It is often beyond the ability of an IT generalist to correctly implement these configurations, so a security provider may be needed to help lock down the network.

2. Review Configuration Regularly

It is very important to review firewall configurations to ensure changes which leave the network vulnerable do not occur. With any IT project, the initial setup of equipment is planned out and documented to be sure it will function as expected, but devices can become neglected over time. Adding a scheduled review of firewall configurations should be part of every company's security plan.

3. Configure Alerts

All NGFW devices have alerts and reports which can be generated from the system. There are even services that take this data and load it into databases for additional reporting and analysis. All companies should set up threat alerts to report directly to internal IT staff. It is also worth considering having a Managed Security Service Provider (MSSP) engaged in monitoring and responding to threats.

4. Keep Software / Signatures Up to Date

As the nature of threats on the Internet are ever-changing; you need to make sure your company's security response is also constantly updated. This is usually accomplished by having a current subscription with the firewall manufacturer and making sure the device is configured to receive updates.

5. Backup Configuration

Most companies have elaborate systems in place to backup data on servers and workstations. Unfortunately, this attention to backup does not typically extend to networking equipment like firewalls. As NGFW devices add more and more features, the configurations quickly become very complex. Manually rebuilding one of these device configurations would lead to significant downtime and lost productivity, so all businesses should manually or automatically back up configurations.

IN SUMMARY

The overall pace of technology advancement has enabled companies to do more with automation, while simultaneously introducing new risks. The struggle between hackers and security providers continues to escalate and requires continuous security improvement to overcome new types of threats. With all this in mind, it is vitally important for all companies to invest in firewall security as a fundamental part of their infrastructure.

About Alan

Alan C. Adcock has been "messing around" with technology for more than 30 years, and yet somehow never gets tired of this ever-changing industry. Alan is CEO of Automated Solutions Consulting Group (ASC Group) in Alpharetta, Georgia. Founded in 1999, ASC Group provides remote network monitoring and management, strategic technology consulting, lifecycle planning, Internet security, data storage and security, and cloud solutions. Many ASC Group clients have been clients for 15+ years.

Alan began his IT career at the age of 17 by working with a local systems integrator as a PC technician, eventually becoming the Senior Systems Engineer and Project Manager at that company. Later, he served as the Vice President of Information Technology for one of Atlanta's largest Real Estate Investment companies. In this role, Alan was responsible for all aspects of technology planning, including computer systems, telecommunications, office equipment, and project management, as well as coordinating technical support and managing a budget for over 155 users.

Alan co-founded Automated Solutions Consulting Group with Gary Smith in 1999 to serve small businesses that needed affordable CRM software solutions and dependable networks to automate their operations. Upon the death of Mr. Smith in 2007, Alan re-focused ASC Group exclusively on network engineering solutions for multi-server, multi-site organizations. ASC Group has since evolved into a full-service network services provider, and serves small-to-midsize businesses, medical practices, private schools and non-profit organizations in the greater Atlanta area.

While working with clients, Alan has seen first-hand the challenges posed by increasingly complex security and compliance demands. Today's smaller organizations have to be prepared to face the same (or greater) threats as large corporations, and ASC Group's goal is to bring big company technology solutions down to the small business level.

Alan grew up in Roswell, Georgia, and is a graduate of Georgia Tech. He currently resides in Woodstock, Georgia, with his wife and son.

CHAPTER 25

CYBER SECURITY IN HEALTHCARE
– CAT AND MOUSE GAME!

BY DAN EDWARDS

Cybersecurity vulnerabilities pose risks for every healthcare provider and their records represent an extremely attractive target for cyber criminals. Imagine having your entire identity stolen. Not one piece of information, but everything tied to you including your social security number, business tax ID, credit card information, retirement, personal and business bank accounts – swiped out from under you and in the hands of a global criminal community for sale on the black market. Reeling from the personal loss, you also uncover that you have lost your entire patient database, patients personal information, financial records, and all of the files your practice has ever produced or compiled. This is identity theft and a breach all in one criminal act . . . while you slept!

A data breach can be far reaching. Your business and personal life would come to a screeching halt while you focus and invest an enormous amount of time, money, effort, and energy trying to restore your credit, finances and good reputation. If your money was gone, how quickly could you recover to pay employees and vendors?

If that was not enough, as if to add insult to injury.... with your stolen identity, the criminal has now used it to pull off other criminal acts. The effects of a single, successful cyber-attack can have far-reaching implications. Could your business survive a front-page news story or the stigma about how you or your practice breached the data of hundreds or thousands of people? Though you might be "innocent until proven guilty" in the justice system, you are "guilty until proven innocent" in the media.

MEDICAL RECORDS ARE MORE VALUABLE THAN CREDIT CARD OR SOCIAL SECURITY NUMBERS

As technology evolves, healthcare providers are finding themselves held to higher cyber security standards to protect themselves in the middle of cyber warfare. Data breaches and hacking-related incidents are not new, however cyber-crime today is becoming more hostile and aggressive especially in relation to the pirating of medical records. Gone are the days where it was just a technology issue. The challenge for IT companies working in healthcare is that they must improve protection without impeding patient care. The severity and regular occurrence of breaches requires security be actively managed.

Healthcare records are currently one hundred times more valuable than credit card or social security numbers according to Poneman Institute's study from 2015 and yield bigger payoffs to data thieves. A cybercriminal will post this information for sale on the dark web (electronic black market) where it can go for upwards of $300 a record, which causes the average small practice to be worth over $500,000. The stolen records with the detailed personal information can lead to credit card fraud, insurance fraud, and identity theft. According to the InfoSec Institute, "Companies operating in the Healthcare sector are a privileged target because of the wealth of personal data they manage, that represents a precious commodity in the criminal underground.

It seems as though the smaller medical or dental practice has a surprisingly less concern for cybercrime and many have an opinion that they fall "under the radar." They oftentimes lack either the resources or belief that an investment is necessary to properly protect their patient data and secure their computers. In addition, it is routine for small businesses to have passwords shared across employees as well as having insecure passwords. It is also commonplace to leave the door open to hackers when there is no protocol to manage user accounts and maintain passwords when an employee leaves.

In this digital age, patients are much better educated and expect to use the Internet when communicating with their doctors. They also assume the provider has taken the necessary steps and deployed suitable measures to "securely" capture, and store their personal information. This means we can see new challenges on the horizon with the Patient-Provider relationships, as they face much more sophisticated security trends.

THE COSTS OF A BREACH AND "THE FALLOUT"

These days anyone watching the news will hear breaches come in many forms and that they are happening at an alarming rate. Criminals are stepping up their game and the breaches are becoming common. The scary part is there are thousands more we do not hear in the news. In the case of a computer contracting malware, criminals can extract information either manually or through an automated data grab. Thus, every Internet connection may be a target to criminals; they do not discriminate on your business size. Not only can breaches come in different forms, they execute them in diverse ways. In fact, large majorities of data breaches derive from human error or perpetrated by a disgruntled employee. Without a forensic audit, it is almost impossible to tell if a breach has occurred or how damaging the breach may be.

Cybercriminals do not just send fraudulent emails and set up fake websites, they also embark on phone call scams. They know your name and other personal information from public directories before calling, so it is easy to trick you into gaining access to your computer. One of the most common scams was the Microsoft Telephone Tech Support. Last year we heard from a medical office that received a call from someone claiming to be from "Microsoft" Tech Support. They stated there was a problem with their computer and offered a solution that required remote access. The office gave this fake "Microsoft" criminal remote access into their system and immediately noticed him starting to access files. Thankfully, they took quick action and disconnected the server from the internet before calling us in. They had a great cyber liability insurance policy in place, which covered a forensic data audit. This protected them from having to pay the high fees of this type of inspection not to mention the fines, penalties or the embarrassment of a breach. Luckily, the audit revealed that no patient information had been compromised or stolen.

Whether it is internal or external you should also be protecting yourself from your own employees. Noticeably, there is a lack of basic employee training in the workplace (especially small-to-medium-sized businesses) on how to identify potential data breach opportunities. It is extremely common for a breach to occur when an employee surfing the web visits an infected website or opens an infected email. From here several things may occur, such as allowing malware to infiltrate the computer as well as creating fraudulent pop-ups. Usually the damage starts with the "click" as the malware/virus software downloads and anticipates your next move making the situation worse as the user attempts to exit the pop-ups. It becomes imperative to block these attacks at the initial level as a much more threatening breach may ensue such as the extraction or deletion of data, ransomware or keyloggers (recording keystrokes). The list is endless and you cannot outsmart these hackers. Many businesses overlook that a breach can also occur because of a computer or disk theft, weak password policy or a lost backup drive.

Recently, a dental practice contacted our firm for help with the CryptoLocker Ransomware that had infected their network. The malware had encrypted all of their patient data and x-rays, leaving them unable to view any patient records, receivables or schedule. The first line of defense was to restore their data to a prior point before the computer was infected. The office had been keeping good backups, however the outdated solution did not include a collection of multiple restore points (the ability to roll their data back to an earlier version). This was their downfall because CryptoLocker was now on all of their external hard drives. Feeling like they had no other options, the doctor paid the ransom via "bitcoins" (digital payment currency) and received a decryption code. Sometimes the code works and sometimes it does not as many codes have less than a 120-hour life from the point of infection. Unfortunately, for them the encryption key had expired and criminals do not offer a money back guarantee. As as a result, they lost most of their information.

Ransomware danger is on the rise and the one who takes the most precautionary approach is less likely to suffer the consequences of such attacks. The number of businesses that operate without a solution that will protect them in the face of any disaster is shocking. A backup is only good if you can restore from it and even better if you can keep working in the face of adversity.

Unlike with credit cards, victims of a healthcare breach where their medical identity was stolen may not simply cancel their accounts with relatively little harm occurring. There is a financial and a medical impact. The outlook for medical identity theft victims is far more severe, paying on average $13,500 in addition to a staggering 200 hours of their time in resolving any problems with their identities or credit. Yet less than 10% of these victims actually achieve their desired results after contributing both time and money.

In certain cases, thieves have used stolen medical identities to obtain their own medical care or drugs for little or no cost to them. The problem lies not only with potential insurance fraud but can have serious implications for the patient's future healthcare if the criminal's medical care ends up on the victim's medical record. They could have to endure things such as increasing insurance costs, and implications that are even more serious if the patient is in need of emergency care and their medical record was inaccurate because of the imposter.

The cost and negative consequences of a breach is very excessive beyond the large legal fees and fines including personally-funded credit monitoring for every breached patient record. The road to recovery can be quite sobering to remediate and unfortunately, it will permanently tarnish your most prized asset.... your reputation. No practice wants to be in the news because of a data breach and no patient wants to continue with a provider that let him or her down and can no longer trust. While the breach may cause a negative impact on patient confidence there can be an even greater negative result if not mediated with the utmost competence. The Internet plays a key role in permanent reviews that will follow you into the future for anyone to see. All these factors combined could very easily devastate even a strong business.

FLEXIBLE SECURITY SOLUTIONS – DO NOT PLAY WITH FIRE!

To ensure the highest security possible for both your practice and patients, any security plans must be put together to remain extremely flexible in concept. With technology constantly changing and expanding, the solution that worked last year or even last month may not be applicable down the road without added solutions. Though a healthcare practice may comply with HIPAA's security regulations to the letter, they need the ability to quickly respond when new threats arise that may require the introduction or change of a security product they are currently using.

For example, an ***extremely common mistake*** in both personal and business computer users is the use of an anti-virus program alone to provide full protection. To add insult to injury they commonly purchase an underpowered product that is either cheap or free. I cannot tell you how many times I see business owners purchase on price and not value. Anti-virus alone will only provide protection from a very narrow range of threats. The "right" anti-virus is necessary but needs to be included in conjunction with layered technologies including, but not limited to, Business class firewall, anti-malware, spam protection, and web filtering solutions. Just recently, the technology behind anti-virus changed significantly to catch viruses and ransomware on a whole new level. When the infrastructure of something like anti-virus changes, you shift also. This is what I mean by flexible. Anti-virus is no longer one-size-fits-all, some companies have figured out how to make a much superior anti-virus product and the technology companies are taking advantage to keep their customers safe.

In a recent survey of 300 organizations, there was an average use of eleven different security technologies put in place to ensure their data safety; this is the new norm of modern businesses. You may wish to create an incident response team which follows a preset and thorough plan wherein if any breach is detected, you will be able to respond both quickly and efficiently, therefore minimizing any impact on a practice as well as the patients. There should be a culture built within the walls of any practice, clinic, or hospital in which data security is commonplace in your daily work.

Cyber Liability Insurance has come a long way, however most professionals seem to know that it exists and can be an add-on to their current business and liability policy. Keep in mind, as with any insurance, not all policies are equal, therefore it is suggested you compare companies to obtain complete coverage. As insurers are continuing to learn what to expect they have begun to help reduce costs by encouraging a quick response that lowers losses and underwrite the risks more effectively. When shopping for coverage consider key components such as Rogue Employee, Network Security, Privacy Liability, Privacy Breach Notification, 1st Party Crime with EFT, Public Relations & Crisis management, Regulatory Defense, Cyber Threats and Extortion, as well as System Damage and Business Interruption.

Here is a story that illustrates how cyber insurance helped where a Zeus malware configuration targeted a seventeen-person Medical office. In this attack, Zeus captured a screenshot of their payroll services web page when a user infected with the Trojan visited the website. This allowed Zeus to steal the user id, password, company number and the icon selected by the user for the image-based authentication system. As a result, the insurance company covered the $28,333 loss from the illegal use of that stolen information.

DON'T DESPAIR – THERE ARE SOLUTIONS THAT WORK – PHYSICAL, NETWORK AND TECHNICAL

Though there is a high and growing threat for hackers to breach medical records of any practice, clinic, or hospital, you can successfully protect yourself and the security of your patients in many ways.

The best place to start is to collaborate with a **Managed IT Service Provider** (MSP) that understands HIPAA and the best practices to prevent data breaches. This is not your average "IT Guy or Company." A well-delivered MSP can help deal with the day-to-day operations to keep your security locked down. An "IT guy" is someone who shows up after the breach has happened charging you thousands of dollars to get you out of the mess. An MSP uses products to help you lockdown things such as where employees can surf the web, and monitor all outgoing and incoming traffic for threats. They will have a HIPAA risk assessment and training of employees the same as a healthcare practice is required to do. This will be a great asset in fighting cybercrimes. This allows you to put your security in the hands of professionally-trained experts that will stand by your side to make sure data breaches and downtime do not happen. Here are some additional guidelines that should definitely be in place at all times:

The HIPAA Security Rule requires that all employees receive HIPAA security training on how to protect patient information and is a huge factor in preventing accidental breaches and it needs to include an annual training update. Make sure that this includes information on responsible Internet usage and best practices. Frequent reminders are crucial to make data safety commonplace within the company and you need to implement an Acceptable Use Policy (AUP) as a contract between yourself and your employees, which states the rules and regulations of Internet and computer usage within your office. This will reinforce the training provided. In most cases, an untrained employee on Internet usage ends up being the open door to the hack.

It is required that you conduct a HIPAA risk assessment and I highly recommended that an independent HIPAA consultant complete this. It should include a cyber risk assessment detailing the condition of your current security policies. The problem is many offices that perform the risk assessment stop there and do not follow through on remediation and solutions.

It is important that you are able to audit who has accessed your network. You will want to make sure that your business class firewall not only protects you but also that you can get regular audit logs showing attempted and hopefully not-successful hacking attempts. The best Business Class Firewalls have Intrusion Prevention Systems and are a great investment in protecting your data. These technologies will block many dangerous viruses and malware from wreaking havoc on your systems.

The use of Active Directory will both secure the network and implement both auditing and logging capabilities. It authenticates and authorizes all users and computers in a domain type network. This is what allows you to maintain and lock out any previous employees from the network and everything they could access.

Look beyond anti-virus with the additional protection against malware, malicious emails and all other threats with Advanced DNS Protection. This blocks employees, (accidentally or on purpose), from accessing any potentially dangerous websites. A company policy prohibiting the use of business computers for personal reasons should be in place at all times.

While Backup and Disaster recovery will not prevent a breach of security, it definitely plays a role in how quickly you can recover and get back to work. This is where the downtime comes into play and measures how soon you can attend to patients, as well as access financial data and medical records. To begin, ensure that you possess a top-of-the-line backup system that can double as a "spare server" with less distraction and downtime and includes an offsite backup with numerous restore points. A word of caution, regularly test the restore capabilities to ensure it is reliable. You do not want to find out when you need it that it has not been working. I am often shocked and saddened at how often the backup solution takes a back seat to all other business decisions, when in actuality it is one of the most important decisions you will make to protect your livelihood in the chance disaster occurs. Disasters also come in many shapes and sizes. . . Backup it up, and back it up again, onsite and in the cloud.

You will want to keep all of your servers, workstations and devices up-to-date with the latest critical and security patches for the operating system and all other software. It is essential to note that support and critical updates are no longer available for both Windows XP and Windows 2003 server. The same will be true in April 2017 when Windows Vista lifecycle will end and no longer receive security patches. The phrase "sitting duck" comes to mind. No more security patches means new threats will come knocking at your door because there are no fixes to stop them from coming through the operating system.

Investigate and purchase Cyber Liability Insurance. In the event of an attack the insurance may cover the cost of a breach completely or partially. Keep in mind that as with any insurance, not all policies are equal, therefore compare companies speaking with carriers about what exactly they do and do not cover. You do not want to be deemed an "exclusion" in your time of need.

YOU DO NOT HAVE TO GO-IT-ALONE: GET A PARTNERSHIP!

After considering both the extensive risk and high cost brought to healthcare practices, clinics or hospitals through cybercrimes, it is very important to note that immediate action be taken to protect yourself and your patients from a traumatic breach that could very well leave you bankrupt. Medical records are some of the highest valued materials available on the dark web, therefore bringing high risks to any size practice. As we have discussed, breaches occur very easily and quickly, in a large number of ways and with varying degrees of seriousness. As a healthcare provider, you are constantly striving to improve quality of patient care, and the assumption is made you will do the same to protect your patients' information.

Security plans should be put in place and remain flexible and it should become commonplace for secure device usage to occur in a practice. You can protect both yourself and your patients in many ways. First, hire a Managed Service Provider whose primary focus is to manage the network 24/7. Collaborating with a security expert focused on making your business a cyber secure operation saves you a lot of grief and gives you time to focus on excellent patient care. Developing a comprehensive security plan requires the full time attention of people, planning, processes, organizational structures and technology, and it should be seamless. A Managed Service Provider is constantly monitoring and responding to danger alerts while you continue to treat your patients and long after your workday is over. Everything, all of it boils down to a single question. . .

HOW SECURE ARE YOU WILLING TO BE?

About Dan

Dan Edwards is the founder and CEO of Pact-One Solutions an award-winning Managed Service Provider based in Las Vegas, with additional locations in San Francisco, Los Angeles, and San Diego. Dan has worked in the Technology Industry for 20 years and has a passion for providing optimized technology solutions for businesses.

After starting Pact-One in 2003, Dan saw the value in gaining the training necessary to better serve his clients and began his quest for changing the nature of how small-to-medium businesses use technology. With natural born leadership and integrity, Dan expanded the business and today Pact-One has more than 30 employees. Dan has always seen a value in hiring the best team and to surround himself with the smartest people to better serve his clients.

Pact-One believes in being a true business partner with its clients by focusing on managed IT services. This means every decision and meeting with the client is focused around how to make their business better through the use of technology while keeping them protected and secure. With many healthcare-related clients, Pact-One has focused on both HIPAA and security to allow their clients to sleep easier at night.

Dan and Pact-One enjoy giving back to charities, through donations and volunteering, such as "Give Kids a Smile," TeamSmile, "CDA Cares", and "Mission of Mercy (MOM)." The Arizona Dental MOM recognized him as a Lead Charter Member from 2012–2014 with great appreciation, compassion and dedication in his role. It has been a passion of his to "give back to the community."

When Dan isn't busy with his many on-going projects, he spends his downtime with his wife Lisa and daughter Danielle traveling, hiking, and golfing, as he finds the balance of work and life extremely important.

You can connect with Dan at:
- Dan@pact-one.com
- http://www.pact-one.com
- https://www.linkedin.com/in/edwardsdan
- https://twitter.com/PACT_ONE
- 702-492-6105 x221

CHAPTER 26

CYBERSECURITY FOR LAW FIRMS
– CREATING A SOUND CORPORATE SECURITY POLICY

BY ILAN SREDNI, CEO
– PALINDROME CONSULTING

There is a distinct difference between compliance and security.

Law firms are known for taking every step possible to ensure attorney/ client privilege. After all, if they didn't, that would be a costly mistake. This is necessary, of course, but is it the only thing they really have to focus on? Certainly not! Without having time-tested, strong cybersecurity policies and practices in place, law firms are playing a riskier game than they may have ever imagined—one that may land them on the defense. Confidential information in the wrong hands—even if it was stolen or lost in error—is a very costly mistake.

Law firm managers need to be as diligent about security as they are about compliance. This involves taking the initiative to follow the best practices through training and education of staff, as well as having the proper technologies in place to stop a cybercriminal from finding an entry into the system. By ignoring the importance of cybersecurity, you are inviting in the potential for fines and penalties, in addition to possibly violating the attorney/client privilege that is so important to clients and attorneys alike.

In March 2012, Jeffrey Brandt, a well-known law firm IT professional and blogger, wrote an article titled When Good Enough—Isn't. In the October 2011 report from the International Legal Technology Association (ILTA) article, we find some staggering statistics that highlight the great risk law firms are taking. While it is a few years later now, these key findings and statistics remain more accurate than not:

- 64% of firms **do not** have intrusion prevention tools
- 61% of firms **do not** have intrusion detection tools
- 58% of firms **do not** encrypt laptops
- 76% of firms **do not** automatically encrypt content-based email
- 78% of firms **do not** issue encrypted USB drives
- 86% of firms **do not** use or require two-factor authentication
- 87% of firms **do not** use any laptop tracking technology

It may be easy to not "pay attention" to these details right away; however, when an emergency occurs and you realize that they could have saved a firm time, money, and reputation by having them in place, suddenly their importance is highlighted quickly and afterthought indeed becomes 20/20.

Instead of reactionary steps, why not advocate proactive measures? That is what I'm going to walk you through in this chapter—what you can do, exactly, to focus on cybersecurity as much as you focus on compliance.

CREATING A CORPORATE SECURITY POLICY

A little planning upfront goes a long way in the end.

A Corporate Security Policy (CSP) is a document that will help highlight that you've taken the necessary preventive measures to significantly reduce the risk of having data and information on your network compromised by a cybercriminal who found an entrance in. As we have come to learn, the criminal enterprise is very sophisticated and many times run just like a Fortune 500 business. Today's criminals are crafty and patient, and smart enough to know not to waste their time trying to get into a system that has implemented a high level of defense.

Through the creation of a CSP, you will be laying out a clearly-defined plan that tells employees what they should do and should not do in case of a cyber breach on the system.

The "Do" List includes:

- Activate the incident response team (IRT)
- Establish a "privileged" reporting and communication channel
- Use independent cyber security and forensic experts
- Stop additional data loss
- Secure evidence
- Preserve all computer logs
- Clearly document the data breach, who, what, when, where and if possible, how
- Consider possibly involving law enforcement and/or regulators
- Determine your legal, contractual, and insurance notification obligations
- Interview personnel involved
- Change security access and passwords
- Remove remote access from the compromised systems

The "Do NOT" List (unless an IT expert tells you otherwise) includes:

- Ignore the incident
- Probe computers and affected systems
- Turn off computers and affected systems
- Image or copy data or connect storage devices/media to affected systems
- Run antivirus programs or utilities
- Reconnect affected systems

Times of cyber breaches are times of stress and panic; however, the degree is lessened when preparations are in place and everyone knows what to do. One of the things that many decision makers for law firms (although they are not alone in this) often say is, "Ilan, we are considering cyber insurance, so all of this may be a bit much. Why do we need that?" This is why:

Cyber insurance policies require that certain safeguards and steps be in place, showing that businesses are taking all logical and practical steps to prevent cyber attacks.

One thing we can rely on is that most people are not pleased to pay for insurance that may not solve their problem should they have to file a claim. This brings us back to the Corporate Security Policy. With this in place, you will be covering what is necessary in order to hopefully prevent a breach. However, in this world where nothing is 100% certain, if one happens to take place, it will show that safeguards and good faith effort were in place, which will lead to a much smoother claim filing process (if it is necessary). We have also found a direct correlation between law firms that take the right steps in protecting themselves and reduced insurance costs.

COMPONENTS FOUND IN A CSP

A well designed and thought out CSP will factor in everything that exists in today's shifting workplace environment—an environment where technology plays a critical role.

With a thoughtful, well executed CSP, law firms are showing their commitment to cybersecurity, which will always have beneficial long-term results. If there is a technology crash, they can return to a fully-functional status more quickly. If there happens to be a breach, they know how to take effective action at a quicker pace because everyone knows their role and responsibility.

The ideal situation will always be that nothing unwelcomed ever happens, and to do that, there are eight specific actions that law firms can take to increase their chances for success. These are all clearly defined in the CSP, which is why that document is so critical. To create this living policy—one that changes as threat landscapes change—using the professional expertise of a company such as Palindrome Consulting makes the difference. We understand all the nuances and keep up with ever-changing cybersecurity on a daily basis. It's our job to do this and it's what we focus on each and every day, 24/7, through the use of our experts and sophisticated, advanced technology that compliments clients' needs.

The nine items listed out here are a must for every business who wants to be serious about preventing cybersecurity risks.

1. Encryption

Quite often and unwisely, laptops and mobile devices are not encrypted. This means that any correspondence you have through emails or data you review is at risk of being exposed! For example, if you found a stolen laptop you could grab its hard drive, use another device and read it—but not if it's encrypted. Then it becomes significantly more difficult, if not possible.

2. Not all "clouds" have a silver lining

Storing information on the cloud is something that's exciting for people to think about today, as it makes a lot of sense for both storage and cost effectiveness. However, there are differences between the various cloud services out there and not all of them offer the same level of protection. Hackers want to break into these cloud services and if they are successful, they will have hit the jackpot for information. Most bar associations do give minimal standards that a firm who is going to use cloud storage must adhere to, but you really want to factor in many things and how they will pertain to your law firm, including:

- Is the main cloud server kept in the US or abroad, or even out of state?
- Data encryption?
- Who else may access your data?
- What about backup and recovery?

All of these things need to be considered, as they are paramount to law firms choices for protecting clients' data. Many law firms even go a step further by having clients sign an acknowledgement that their confidential data will be stored on the cloud. That doesn't eliminate their risks should a hack occur, but it is another step to ensure that their clients are as informed about their practices as possible.

3. Bring Your Own Device (BYOD)

I like to think of BYOD as the "new wild west." A BYOD environment allows for employees to use their own devices for managing and communicating confidential information. It's intriguing, but it's very risky! We often find situations where clients are enamored with the idea, but they don't take the proper precautions or really think it through. How do you ensure privacy of confidential information? How do you gauge how to pay hourly wage employees? What happens if a device is stolen? In order to offer solutions to these pressing questions, law firms that embrace BYOD must make sure they use encryption, plus have the ability to wipe a device clean from a remote location—for both a theft and if an employee leaves the company.

4. Vendor management

Law firms, just like any business, want to find the best value for their money when it comes to the vendors they choose to work with. There is something that should trump good value for the buck, though, and that is the vetting process of vendors. When you are entrusting someone with confidential data, you want to know their exact records, methods, and policies within their own organizations to determine how effectively they can protect what you will be sharing with them. And if they have access to specific parts of your data base, this becomes even more important. A good value means nothing if it could lead to your law firm closing down due to fines, penalties, and a lack of client trust.

5. Training

As essential as technology is to prevent cyber problems from occurring, it is rendered ineffective when the employees who use the technology are not trained on the proper policies. The human factor brings along bad habits from how people use technology at home or how they used it at a previous employer. Through training we offer a way for employees to gain knowledge about the process and then to apply it! This includes:
- Applicable communications with them to reiterate policies and expectations
- Retraining on a regular basis, making sure that staff turnover doesn't lead to weaknesses within the system
- Proper email protocol, including opening up unknown attachments, phishing emails, etc.

6. Password policy

The importance of a good password cannot be emphasized enough and with good reason. It is a non-negotiable! This will require buy-in from the managing partners of any firm in order to be properly implemented. The responsibility of creating the password does fall on the users, but the network administrator should put the right rules in place. Password best practices are discussed on multiple chapters in this book, please refer to those.

7. Wi-Fi awareness

It is easier to get tricked into joining an unsafe Wi-Fi network than what most people think. As a test, I created a Wi-FI network one time that had a title that included both a hotel name on it and "fastest free Wi-Fi" in its title. Within 40 minutes, there were a 147 people that had connected to it. 67 of them went to their banking websites. 83 connected to their office. 34 had open and shared folders on their laptop easily read by anyone on the Wi-Fi network. All this happened because they just assumed they were safe. What if I had been the bad guy and not the good guy out to prove a point? You must do your due diligence when connecting to a Wi-Fi. Factor in all these things, as they will help negate the risks:

- Did you get the hotel Wi-Fi password and network ID from the hotel itself?
- Are you using a VPN (Virtual Private Network) to connect to your office when you use a public Wi-Fi?
- If available, use your Wi-Fi hot spot on your cellular device, as that will be safer and information you view will be encrypted.

8. Business continuity and Disaster Recovery plans

Business Continuity encompasses Disaster Recovery, Backups and even business succession planning. It provides the strategy and process involved to make sure your company survives the loss of key individuals, data, equipment, or facilities. Disaster Recovery typically refers how companies recover from large scale disasters, like an earthquake or the terrorist attacks. The basic building block of both is not only how you backup your data, but how quickly and where you can restore it. Take into account onsite, off-site, backup's frequency, total, incremental options, their pros and cons. Both business continuity plans and disaster recovery plans determine how a company will keep functioning after a disruptive event until its normal facilities and capabilities are restored.

9. Preparation and trial tests

Do not be hesitant to test any aspects of your CSP to make sure that it is working as you envision it should. This includes looking at:

- Employee use: are they doing what you have asked of them? This would include BYOD policies, password changes, and Wi-Fi awareness.
- System failures: does your data recovery process actually work? You need to be able to gain access to all data to be fully operational in the designated amounts of time you've indicated in a recovery plan.
- Business awareness: are your vendors the safest choices for your firm, and is your cloud service proactive in efforts to ward off attackers? When you rely on others to perform at your best, it is wise to make sure you know what those others are up to when it comes to your security.

Not heeding the importance of cybersecurity in the highly competitive and confidentiality driven world of practicing law is unwise. Quite literally, nothing good can come of it. The more you embrace security as a necessity for your law firm, the better you'll be able to conduct your business and serve your clients' needs.

TAKE ACTION TODAY

Waiting another day to create an effective Corporate Securities Policy may make you a day late, which will impact your bottom line, client retention, and reputation.

About Ilan

Ilan Sredni has been an IT professional for almost 25 years and prides himself in helping small- and-medium-sized businesses (SMBs) achieve the same level of proficiencies. Ilan's company, Palindrome Consulting specializes in working with high-caliber law firms, businesses and medical practices to find IT solutions that help gear them for success in today's world.

Through his company, Palindrome Consulting, Inc., Ilan and his engineers give of their spare time to help out non-profit organizations so they too can receive the benefits of technology and allow them to compete in the marketplace. Ilan is heavily involved in a number of non-profit organizations helping the hungry and needy.

Ilan started his professional career with Pepsi Cola International and quickly moved up the ranks in Corporate America. From there, he joined a government contractor, The Protective Group, as their IT manager and was instrumental in helping set the groundwork for their ISO certifications. Following a short stint in the .com arena, Ilan founded Palindrome Consulting in 1999.

Ilan lives with his wife, Lilian, and their four children in North Miami, Florida.

To learn more about Palindrome Consulting and their Corporate Security Policy, visit the website: www.pciicp.com/csppolicy. Their CSP has the information on it to put into action all of the things discussed.